RAYMOND BRIDGE, author of eight other guides to outdoor sports, has wide outdoor experience ranging from hiking and canoeing to white-water kayaking and expeditionary mountaineering and has lectured and taught these subjects to outdoor groups and at several colleges.

High Peaks & Clear Roads

A SAFE & EASY GUIDE TO OUTDOOR SKILLS

Raymond Bridge

A SPECTRUM BOOK

PRENTICE-HALL, INC., Englewood Cliffs, New Jersey   07632

Library of Congress Cataloging in Publication Data

Bridge, Raymond.
    High peaks & clear roads.

    (A Spectrum Book)
    Bibliography: p.
    Includes index.
      1. Outdoor life.   2. Camping—Outfits, supplies, etc.
I. Title.
GV191.6.B74   796.5   77-14300
ISBN 0-13-387548-2
ISBN 0-13-387530-X pbk.

© 1978 by Prentice-Hall, Inc., Englewood Cliffs, New Jersey   07632

A Spectrum Book

10 9 8 7 6 5 4 3 2 1

Printed in the United States of America

PRENTICE-HALL INTERNATIONAL, INC., *London*
PRENTICE-HALL OF AUSTRALIA PTY. LIMITED, *Sydney*
PRENTICE-HALL OF CANADA, LTD., *Toronto*
PRENTICE-HALL OF INDIA PRIVATE LIMITED, *New Delhi*
PRENTICE-HALL OF JAPAN, INC., *Tokyo*
PRENTICE-HALL OF SOUTHEAST ASIA PTE. LTD., *Singapore*
WHITEHALL BOOKS LIMITED, *Wellington, New Zealand*

Dedicated to the memory of
Kim Wickholm
Sharon Barnes
Stewart Frost
who loved wild places,
cherished the opportunity
to share them with others,
and fought to preserve them.

Contents

part III | **SELF-PROPELLED TRAVEL: AN INTRODUCTION**

Introduction

This is a book about lightweight travel and camping for those rediscovering the spell of the North American landscape. The magic of space is the taproot of the American character. The lure of the western horizon, the rightness of the land, and the sense of the power of the wilderness were major elements in changing the Europeans who came to the United States and Canada into Americans. A reawakening of that sense of limitless potential is part of the reason for the tremendous interest in backpacking, canoeing, cycling, and other forms of self-contained travel in the past few years.

Nothing is quite so renewing after a time spent in civilized pursuits and under civilizing pressures as an encounter with the natural world. It can lend a sense of perspective that is unmatched by contrived entertainments. Such experiences vary from ambitious mountaineering endeavors to quiet bicycle rides on country roads, but they have the common virtue of bringing us back to our sources, of reminding us that we are part of a complex and beautiful environment, richer and more varied than we can imagine. There's a world out there for the finding.

Lightweight camping has the virtue of attending to human

needs that aren't usually well satisfied in our daily lives. It gives the camper healthy exercise in an atmosphere of beauty and quiet, with the opportunity for solitude or companionship, but without the nagging pressures of the office, store, house, school, or factory. It provides for a change of pace, for a few days of living at a more basic and less complicated level, which enables many people to return to their normal activities refreshed. For others, a wilderness experience can give a whole new perspective on life. Open spaces provide us the opportunity for recreation in all senses of the word, from pleasant interludes in our daily lives to a true re-creation of the self.

THE PURPOSE OF THIS BOOK

Modern camping equipment and techniques make life easier for the wilderness wanderer. Properly chosen gear is lightweight and efficient, and it allows camping with minimal impact on the often fragile surroundings the traveler has sought out. The boon to the camper is great, since he or she can make extensive treks with reasonable loads, which would often have required pack animals or laborious relaying a few years ago. At the same time, if it is used correctly, modern equipment enables large numbers of people to enjoy the limited wilderness and open space areas that have been preserved, without degrading them.

This book is an introduction to a number of types of lightweight, self-propelled travel. It discusses equipment extensively, not because equipment is the most important aspect of a backpacking or canoe trip, but because the beginner is faced with decisions about equipment purchases from the time he or she contemplates a first overnight jaunt. Lightweight camping gear is expensive, and bad choices can have ruinous effects on both the budget and the enjoyment of a trip.

A number of excellent books are available on various back-

Figure 1 Wilderness travel offers an experience of a beautiful world remote from the concerns and values of civilization—a place for renewal.

country sports, such as mountaineering or backpacking, but since a lot of the same equipment can be used whether one is kayaking, climbing, or bicycling, it seems worthwhile to consider together items that aren't specific to one type of outdoor activity. A lot of people just starting to do backcountry camping are equally interested in canoeing and backpacking, or mountaineering and cycling, and few of us can afford to have separate sleeping bags or packs for half a dozen different activities. It's useful to consider the requirements of various outdoor sports and forms of travel together, so that, when possible, you can buy equipment suitable for many uses.

The second part of this book discusses general outdoor skills, which are again common to most extended outdoor trips. The skills associated with staying comfortable in the backcountry on mountaineering treks and downriver runs are fairly similar. Though the techniques of travel may be worlds apart, the principles for staying warm and dry, for preparing appetizing meals, and for meeting emergencies are very similar.

Finally, there are a number of chapters introducing some of the specific forms of travel and recreation in the open spaces and wilderness of North America: hiking, backpacking, cycling, winter travel, mountaineering, canoeing, and kayaking. I hope that these will be useful both to beginners and to people who are experienced in certain outdoor activities and who are curious about the rudiments of others. References are included for those who want to know more.

I hope that this guide will prove useful to those who yearn to get out into the open spaces. Remember that preservation of the wild and unspoiled places of the country is the responsibility of those who use and love them. There are always many people who either want to exploit the land for short-term personal profit, or simply don't understand the value of anything that doesn't bear the heavy imprint of modern society. There are also many who don't understand the importance of treading lightly on the backcountry, so that it will remain pristine. If you learn to love wild places, don't forget to take the time and trouble to help preserve them.

part
I

GETTING YOUR PACK TOGETHER

chapter | **Pick Up**
1 | **And Go**

For most people interested in lightweight travel, time and opportunity are limited. Distances to favorite spots are often long. Even if the expense of transportation doesn't present difficulties, time usually does. Two days may stretch out to eternity on a working day, but they don't last long on a weekend. For the inveterate outdoorsperson, it's nice to be able to pick up the pack and go on a few minutes' notice.

The simplest way to manage this is to have your pack or storage bags ready beforehand, containing all the essentials you need for a weekend trip except for perishables and the clothes you'll wear. While this plan may need some revision, particularly if you go on many different sorts of jaunts, it can usually be followed at least in part. It has other advantages, too. The most important contents for any wilderness pack or road bag are the emergency items and the things you need for survival or a modicum of comfort in the face of bad weather, unexpected difficulties, and other problems on the trail, river, or road. These are also the items that take a lot of time to remember and get out if you start to think about your trip on Friday evening while your friends are waiting in the car or the kids are yelling for supper: things like the flashlight, raingear, a first-aid kit, insect

7

repellent, or sun cream. If those things are already packed, and you know they're all there, a lot of time and trouble can be saved.

In this chapter, we'll mention some ways of getting off efficiently onto the open road or the trail. Later in the book, there's specific information on different kinds of equipment, camping methods, and so forth. Initial preparation can be one of the biggest obstacles to getting out, however. Making the drive to the trailhead or the canoe put-in on Friday evening may not be too odious, but spending the evening getting ready and *then* making the drive probably will be. If you can hop in the car or onto the bus and go, with a minimum of last-minute preparation, you'll get out far more often. Finally, in looking at the preparation for a trip, the complete novice will find out a lot about camping and outdoor activities.

THE ESSENTIALS

For any particular sort of outdoor activity there are a number of important items one always wants to have along, but they're often easy to forget. Things like a flashlight (or a bicycle lamp or headlamp), raingear, sun cream, and similar items are often left at home, unless a lot of time is taken to check everything over. In most outdoor activities, neglecting small details like this can cause a lot of discomfort, easily turning what would have been a fine trip into a miserable one. Fifty miles of pedaling under the spring sun before reaching a store where one can buy suntan lotion can easily change the following week into pure hell instead of a relaxing vacation. In some cases, particularly on mountaineering and winter trips, small pieces of equipment like this can be the key to survival in an emergency.

The easiest way to be sure that you won't forget the essentials when you're in a hurry to get off, and to speed preparation at the same time, is to keep them in a pack or in a stuff sack,

Figure 2 Getting out into the backcountry requires getting essential equipment together for the trip on which you want to go. You'll enjoy yourself more if you learn to do this efficiently.

ready to go. This is especially easy to do if you're taking pretty much the same sort of trips during a particular time of year, or if you maintain several packs because your different activities require different containers. The principle is also easy to apply to the rest of your equipment, so that it is ready to go in just a few minutes.

For backpacking trips, as an example, it's quite easy to get your pack ready for the next trip when you clean up after the one before. Pots can be cleaned and put back in the pack, the fuel bottle refilled, tent swept out and dried, and everything can be readied for the next excursion. Most food for backpacking trips keeps quite well, so a menu can often be planned and packed well in advance also. It's also much easier to remember items that may need to be replaced, such as batteries or moleskin, right after a trip than after a week or a month has passed. A list can be pinned to the top of the pack to remind you of items which still have to go in before you leave, such as perishables and a map of the place where you're going.

If the trips you take vary somewhat in character, so that

some items can be left at home some of the time, try packing in advance for more severe climates and removing those things that aren't needed just before you leave. These can then be replaced in the pack when you return, so they'll be there the next time. It's easier to remember to leave things behind than to take them. Thus, you might leave your tent packed for the high mountains, but if you head for the desert instead, you can just remove the main part of the tent and take the fly alone.

If you go on many kinds of trips, you may still be able to use a modification of the same scheme. Basic gear for getting along in the outdoors, staying comfortable, and handling emergencies, like the flashlight, first-aid kit, raingear, and such, can go in a pack or stuff sack. Essential overnight gear that would be suitable for any trip might go in another container. Finally, equipment that's peculiar to a particular sport can be packed together. Tool kit, spare tube or tire, leg light, cycling shoes, and the like can be placed in a stuff sack or panniers, ready to be picked up for a bicycle trip, while wet suits, life jackets, and fiberglass or aluminum repair kits are in a dry pack or other bag for canoe or kayak trips. Getting ready for a trip can be fairly simple if this system is established. On getting home from work on Friday evening after receiving a call from a mountaineering friend who proposes a weekend trip, you can grab your bag of normal summer essentials, the overnight sack—together with the map and pieces of fruit the note on it reminds you to add—and your technical climbing gear, if that's appropriate, throw it all in a pack, and be ready to go in ten minutes.

Another simple method for speeding the packing process while assuring that important items won't be forgotten is to make up a series of checklists of items that may be needed on various kinds of trips. The checklist should be complete, though a number of things may not be needed on a particular trip. When packing, the camper can then run down the list as the items are either packed or deliberately left out. Personal lists made in this way can be quite specific, including each piece of equipment or group of things packed together, so that there's far less chance of leaving anything behind than if a general list

Figure 3 Treks to remote areas require more elaborate preparation, but the rewards are worth the effort.

from a book is used. Once thorough lists have been made up, if everything is kept where it can be readily packed up, getting ready for a trip will take only a little longer than it would if the packs were readied beforehand. It is helpful when packing food if a number of food lists, listing all the ingredients necessary for particular menus, are made up in order to simplify shopping trips and food packing.

GETTING READY FOR LONGER TRIPS

Preparing for longer and more elaborate trips naturally requires more thought and care than picking up and going on a weekend jaunt. Since more food will probably have to be carried, equipment has to be considered very carefully to keep weight at a minimum, without sacrificing so much comfort that the trip will cease to be a pleasure. If you're going to more remote areas than can be reached in a weekend, many usually adequate supplies may have to be expanded to suit the needs that may arise. First-aid kits may need to be more elaborate, for example, and repair kits generally need to be much more complete. Lists often have to be reconsidered if you're going to a place with far different conditions than those within a few hours' drive.

These more time-consuming preparations are far less of a burden for longer trips than they would be for those lasting only a couple of days. Much of the enjoyment of an extended camping trip lies in the anticipation and planning of it. The usual list or complete pack will still serve well as a starting point, however, because you can simply go through it and consider each item's adequacy to meet the conditions that will be encountered on the trip.

The careful consideration of each piece of equipment for an extended trip on unfamiliar ground also points up the ease with which it should be possible to assemble a weekend pack for local jaunts, once a little experience has been gained. If you camp on most trips in the mountains or woods near home, it isn't necessary to go through a long and elaborate estimation of what will be necessary. Where good water is fairly easy to come by, the same size water bottle will do perfectly well for day hikes, weekend backpacks, or mountaineering efforts. If it's kept in the side pocket of the pack or in a day bag, then it will always be thrown into the pack out of habit, and if water disinfectant is needed, it can be left ready in some corner pocket. With this general approach, the backcountry camper can always be ready to pick up and go. Once the obstacles of elaborate preparations are eliminated, it's far simpler and more relaxing to actually get off.

BEGINNINGS

The ideal of being able to take off for a weekend in the backcountry on short notice appeals to a lot of people who just don't know how to get started, and it's to these people that the following chapters are directed. In order to have all those bits of equipment ready to toss into the pack, you first have to acquire them. Knowing what to pack requires at least a rudimentary knowledge of outdoor skills. The matter of equipment has to be tackled first, because it must be faced from the start by the novice.

chapter | **What You Need**
2 | **And**
| **What You Don't**

One of the most common mistakes made by beginners in backpacking and other sorts of lightweight camping is to buy equipment designed for much more severe conditions than the novice is ever likely to encounter. This is a particularly unfortunate error for those who don't have much money to spend, since it usually means that other needed items can't be bought. Thus, people are always ending up with expedition-style down parkas before they have suitable clothing for normal weather conditions, with technical ice climbing boots but nothing that is comfortable to hike in, or with tents suitable for winter mountaineering before basic camping equipment is acquired.

Prior to shopping for equipment, the beginner should develop an accurate idea of just what kind of trips he or she will be going on in the next year or so, what conditions will be met, and what kind of gear is necessary to enjoy the experience. If all those excursions will be made during the milder seasons, then articles designed for winter conditions will be unnecessarily heavy and expensive. An outfit that's ideal for the climate of the Canadian Rockies won't be the optimum one for the Southwestern desert. There's a lot of versatility in camping equipment, but the best course is normally to purchase things that are just right for the kind of outing you take most of the time, working out compromise methods and supplemental gear to handle the exceptional trips.

In the following chapters that deal with specific sorts of equipment, the reader will find again and again the advice that the most important step in purchasing gear is analyzing one's own needs. No one else can tell you what sort of trip and what sort of approach will most appeal to you. Experienced people can point out common errors and give advice on the suitability of particular tools for different uses, but you'll have to apply that advice to your own requirements.

You know more than anyone else about your own body and the way it reacts, about your attitudes, and about the degree of comfort that's important to you. Remember to keep both your fears and fantasies subordinate to your judgment, however. If you're usually about as warm or cold as most other people, then sleeping bags and clothing that have served most other people well in particular conditions will probably do nicely for you, too. On the other hand, even if it's your ambition to climb Mount McKinley in winter, get backpacking gear that is suitable for the local hills first. Buy the equipment you need, not the equipment you wish you needed.

APPROACHES

It's worth remembering that the more experienced you become at lightweight camping, the better idea you'll have of which equipment is just right for you and of what you need and what you don't. For this reason alone, it's wise to postpone all your purchases as long as possible. The longer you can wait, the better chance you'll have of avoiding expensive mistakes. Thus, if you can make do with a plastic tube tent for a while, you'll be able to put off buying a tent until you have a more precise idea of your needs. For many of us, purchasing all the camping gear we may eventually want is financially out of the question anyway.

Postponing purchases will enable you to whittle your shopping list down to real essentials. Luxury items like down parkas, insulated booties, and such may never be necessary for you, and they certainly shouldn't take precedence over basics. For the really necessary gear, think about borrowing some things from friends, if you have any who do lightweight camping. Once you've slept out on a chilly night in a sleeping bag with certain characteristics, you'll have a far better idea of what insulation thickness you need. Similarly, if you can manage to borrow a few kinds of packs, bicycle panniers, or whatnot, you'll have a better idea of the merits of various types and how well they suit your purposes when you go out to buy your own.

Renting is another temporary way to obtain many pieces

Figure 4 A skier on a winter camping trip in the Colorado Rockies. Severe weather is often encountered on wilderness trips like this, and it's important to have proper equipment. Many people spend a lot of money on things they don't need, however, neglecting essentials.

of equipment for those who live within a reasonable distance of the larger suppliers of lightweight equipment. Though renting gear is expensive in the long run, it's a good way of gaining experience with different kinds of equipment and of putting off major purchases. In fact, the observant beginner can rapidly become an expert about many aspects of equipment by judicious renting, since the average backcountry traveler is likely to use the same gear for many years, thus having only limited knowledge of other types and of recent developments. Many shops will apply at least some rental fees to the purchase of equipment.

Before making any major purchases, the novice would be wise to study a number of catalogs of manufacturers and mail-order houses and to visit shops in his or her area, to try to get a good idea of what is available, the going prices, and the supposed advantage of different sorts of equipment. Ask the advice of friends who are knowledgeable about the kind of camping you plan to do.

QUALITY AND COST

Though there are quite a few bargains that can be found in lightweight camping equipment, they require some examination on the part of the prospective buyer. As lightweight camping has gained in popularity, there have been a lot of improvements in equipment, but a lot of poorly made junk has become available as well. There are exceptions, but it's usually poor economy to save a few dollars in price on a badly made piece of gear, because it will fall apart in a short period of time, usually just when you're relying on it in a difficult situation. A pack frame which breaks when you are 30 miles from the road can create more than a minor inconvenience. A bicycle pannier that vibrates into the spokes while you are riding down a steep grade at 40 miles an hour could kill you. Other failures may not be so threatening, but they are still annoying. If you do decide to buy equipment of inferior quality, at least be sure that you are really getting a bargain. Saving 15 dollars on a sleeping bag won't be a long-term economy if it lasts only a year or two, instead of ten.

Except for the few real surplus bargains which remain, mainly on clothing, the best savings are usually to be found by buying secondhand equipment, rental stocks from stores, and sale or discontinued items from reputable lightweight equipment shops and manufacturers. Making your own equipment either from scratch or from kits is another way to economize. By shopping carefully and using sources of this type, it's possible to reduce the cost of a good outfit to a fraction of what it would normally cost. Similarly, close examination of one's real needs will often save a lot of money. Many good companies make simple equipment that eliminates a lot of nonessential frills for those on a budget, without degrading basic quality in materials or construction. Thus, large numbers of zippered pockets on packs require a lot of extra sewing labor and a considerable increase in the cost of materials. (Zippers are expensive.) It is usually a better idea to buy a quality pack without the extra pockets rather than a badly sewn one with all the extras.

Good quality camping gear should last through a lot of hard use, and for this reason it usually pays to buy well-made equipment. A decent pack should last a lifetime in normal use (except in abusive mountaineering), and tents and sleeping bags ought to stay around for a decade of fairly regular camping, if they are given decent care. Many last a lot longer. Keep this in mind when you are buying equipment.

Careful selection, postponement of purchases, and a strong touch of the skinflint are the best means of avoiding expensive mistakes in buying lightweight gear. If you can afford to buy a lot of equipment before coming up with the right outfit, then start ordering; you will provide others with a lot of inexpensive secondhand equipment. If you are on a budget, however, take the time and effort to analyze your real needs, and then select items that will last for a while.

chapter 3 | **Clothing**

Clothing for use in the backcountry or on the open road should be reasonably functional, satisfying the basic needs of the human body for protection from the elements as a first priority, with considerations of vanity at least relegated to a secondary role. Those who want outdoor clothing that's both useful and fashionable will usually have to pay well for their tastes, while those less concerned with sartorial considerations in the wilderness may be able to get a lot of their clothes from attic trunks and surplus stores.

Self-propelled travelers living outdoors from a small pack or gear bag need clothing that will keep them comfortable in a wide variety of weather conditions which city life leaves them unprepared for. On many backpacking trips an afternoon may be hot with the sun burning, while the following morning may be rainy, with air temperatures hovering just above the freezing point. Contrasting weather abounds in the favorite haunts of wilderness travelers. In many cases, clothing must also be designated to suit the specific needs of the traveler's activities as well. The cyclist, kayaker, and canoeist, in particular, often need special features in their clothing.

It is probably easiest to consider some of the particular

conditions that clothing needs to fill in various outdoor activities before going on to specifics. By keeping his or her own plans in mind, the novice can easily apply these considerations to particular situations.

INSULATION

The most common function for clothing is to keep the body at a comfortable operating temperature, even in hostile surroundings. The human body has a very complex and sophisticated system for regulating temperatures, but it won't keep the unclothed body comfortable in a cold environment.

The body can be thought of as a heat-producing machine. Heat is a byproduct of all muscular activity, of digestion, and of

Figure 5 Functional outdoor clothing is important, and a number of thin layers are usually more practical than one thick one. This winter climber is wearing a wool shirt, which retains some insulating value even if it gets wet, and wool pants underneath nylon-shell pants. He has a hat, mittens, sweaters, and a shell top in the pack.

basic body metabolism. Heat production can be increased if the body starts to cool. The vital organs of the body are only able to function properly within a very narrow temperature range, and for them to remain at that constant temperature, the heat loss from the body to its surroundings must be in balance with the heat production of the body. If less heat is lost than is produced, the body will start to heat up dangerously, while if heat losses exceed production, the body will begin to cool. The reactions of the body to increased temperature are increased circulation to the skin to allow more heat loss there and sweating to permit cooling by evaporation. When chilled, the body will reduce circulation to the skin and outer layers of tissue, so that less heat can be lost. Other mechanisms also play a part, but these are the primary ones.

To help the body stay warm, we add clothing that will reduce the loss of heat from the skin. For comfort, we need to keep those losses low enough so that circulation, particularly to the hands and feet, doesn't need to be reduced very much; otherwise the extremities feel cold. Except for items like electric socks, however, clothing produces no warmth; it merely assists the body in retaining the heat it produces.

Heat losses can occur in a number of ways, and clothing, to be effective, must work against the kind of loss that's actually occurring. In most outdoor situations where heat loss is a problem, it occurs by transfer of heat from the skin to much colder molecules of air surrounding it. The warmed molecules are then replaced by new cold ones, and the transfer process continues. This transfer is speeded up a great deal if the cold air is driven past the skin by a breeze or wind, producing the now familiar but poorly understood "wind-chill" effect.

The first line of defense against the chilling effects of air should be against the wind or breeze, if there is one. The outer layer of clothing should be relatively windproof when the cold breezes blow, so that the wind-chill element is largely eliminated. Any very tightly woven outer layer will accomplish this. Generally, it's most efficient to have a separate wind shell, at least for the upper body, which can be worn with or without insulation layers; but some campers prefer a jacket with a windtight outer layer. Rain garments may be used to double for a wind shell for some conditions, but the condensation problems associated with coated material usually make this undesirable.

Even after wind circulation has been largely eliminated, air will circulate readily around the warm skin, unless some kind of insulation is used. Virtually all insulation used for normal clothing—and most other earthbound purposes—consists of some sort of matrix containing a lot of little air chambers. Air is an excellent insulator, providing it is held in small compartments that prevent the molecules from freely circulating. Insulators consisting largely of air are very practical, because they consist mainly of empty space, greatly reducing weight. In many cases they are quite compressible as well, so they can be stuffed into small spaces when not in use. Insulators using a matrix of air pockets vary slightly in effectiveness, depending on how small the individual chambers are and how effectively the separation prevents circulation. Basically, however, the insulation provided by such a garment is directly proportional to the thickness of the layer. An inch of wool provides pretty much the same amount of insulation as an inch of down, polyester, foam, fiberglass matting, or sheepskin. Other considerations make one or another better, but the insulation value of the dry material in fairly still air is the same.

OTHER CONSIDERATIONS

A lot of different factors go into the choice of good outdoor clothing, but it is just as well to dispel myths about the magical properties of various insulators first. There are other forms of heat loss besides that by cold air, and other kinds of protection that clothes may be called on to provide. Miracle insulators are not available, however, and you should be suspicious of over-blown claims.

The second most important type of heat loss for the out-doorsperson is caused by water, and it can take many forms. The most severe losses are the result of immersion in cold water, as may happen to a capsized boater, to a hiker slipping into a stream, or to a backpacker on a river crossing. The rapidity with which the body can be chilled in cold water is truly astounding; you can become dangerously cold in just a few minutes in water that doesn't at first seem particularly cold. For this reason, white-water boaters customarily wear neoprene-foam wet suits much of the time, and they are essential for safety whenever there's any serious risk of a dunking in water below 50°F (10°C) or pro-longed immersion in water below 59°F (15°C). A person already chilled will be brought to a dangerous state even more rapidly.

A wet suit is made of neoprene rubber blown full of bubbles more or less closed off from one another. Thus, water can't readily circulate through it, and since it's tightly cut and stretchy, circulation under the suit is also limited. The skin gets wet, but a layer of warmed water is held in place, and the layer of neoprene limits conduction to the water outside. A wet suit is very effective in protecting the body against the chilling effects of cold water, if the correct thickness and coverage are chosen, but it's important to note that water temperatures never fall below 32°F (0°C), since some articles have touted foam for winter sleeping bags on the wet-suit principle. Putting on a frozen wet suit is sheer misery, and foam makes a poor choice for insulation against cold air.

For the traveler on land, immersion is unlikely except in special circumstances, but cooling by water can still be a major problem. The most dangerous conditions for producing hypo-thermia, or chilling of the body's core, occur, not during ex-treme cold temperatures, but during wet, windy weather a little above freezing. A hiker caught out in cold, wind-driven rain may be chilled by the cold water running over his skin, and by the evaporative cooling as the water goes back into the vapor stage. The greatest problem, however, is usually caused by the loss of the insulating value of wet clothing. Wet clothes are never very good insulators, but some materials are worse than others in their vulnerability to moisture. Cotton is virtually worthless as an insulator when it gets wet, and it dries slowly, feeling clammy and often abrasive until it's completely dry. Thus, while cotton makes a good material for some shell clothing and for hot-weather wear, it's a very poor choice for basic clothing when cold, wet conditions may be encountered.

Keeping clothes dry can often be a major problem, because the body contains a lot of water, and the skin is maintained in a fairly moist condition. Thus, even when you're not apparently sweating, evaporation from the skin is always taking place except when the air next to the skin is completely saturated with water vapor. One of the consequences is that when you're out in cold rain, putting on a waterproof garment that will keep water from getting to the clothing from the outside may cause heavy condensation of the moisture that has evaporated from the skin on the inside of the rain garment. This condensation may soak the clothing as effectively as rain. Condensation occurs because the warm air next to the skin can take up a lot of water, but when it hits the cold coated material, it deposits much of that water like dew. The situation is obviously made far worse if the outdoorsperson actually starts to sweat. Partial solutions to this problem are always being devised, some more effective than others, but none are wholly effective. As a consequence, for most cold-weather situations, it's best to wear clothing that dries fairly easily and that retains some of its insulating value even when it gets wet.

The traditional outdoor clothing material that copes best with the wet-cold problem is wool. Wool retains far more insulating capacity when it gets wet than cotton, and it tends to dry from the skin out, rather than the reverse. It's still preferred by many for long underwear and for pants, shirts, and sweaters for cold weather. Good quality wool underwear is very soft, and it bothers very few people's skins.

A number of synthetic materials have also proven very effective for their properties in combined conditions of moisture and cold. Acrylic pile has been successfully used for general garments and underwear, and the latter has also been made from bulked acrylics. Polyester batting, such as Fiberfill II and Polarguard, is widely used for insulation in more heavily insulated garments. Polyester insulated garments are discussed more completely later in the chapter.

THE LAYER PRINCIPLE

For most outdoor wear, it's best to carry a number of relatively light layers of clothing, rather than a few heavy ones. For example, a wool shirt, a wool sweater, and a windbreaker might be taken, instead of one heavy jacket of the same total weight. Several layers of clothing permit much more versatility and better temperature control than a few heavy ones. The sweater and windbreaker can be taken off after you warm up on the trail, while all you can do with the jacket, short of removing it, is to unbutton the front. Your back may still be hot and sweating, though your chest is chilly.

Another reason for layering is that many pockets of fairly still air are trapped between the layers, providing extra warmth without extra weight. In general, several layers of clothing are warmer for their weight than a single heavier layer made of similar material. Down garments designed for very cold high-altitude conditions are an exception to this rule, but for basic outdoor clothing, the layer principle is a good one to follow.

Layering clearly also permits the outdoorsperson to get by with fewer pieces of expensive, specialized clothing. If you're going out in a little colder weather, an extra sweater can simply be added to the layers, rather than switching from one down parka to a heavier one.

SHELL CLOTHING

The outer layer of an onion is the one intended to protect the more tender inner ones. Shell garments serve the same purpose. They're usually made of plain, tightly woven fabric, providing little or no insulation. The fabric and the design depend on individual preferences and the conditions that the shell is intended to protect against.

Shell clothing intended solely for protection from wind is most commonly made from lightweight, close-woven nylon fabric. Such garments are relatively inexpensive, take up very little space, weigh next to nothing, and break the wind very well. They're not much help in the rain and have little abrasion

Figure 6 Uninsulated shell parkas like the ones worn by these igloo builders serve to turn the wind and weather. Insulating layers are worn underneath when they are needed.

resistance, but a nylon windbreaker can be a very useful garment. It dries quickly if it does get wet. Wind pants are less commonly used, except for mountaineering, though they can be helpful to cyclists as well. Rain pants often serve well as wind pants also, since ventilation is normally less of a problem in the high wind conditions where wind pants are needed, and since condensation is less of a problem on the lower body anyway. Some wind parkas come with coated fabric as a second layer on the hood and shoulders only, on the theory that modest amounts of rain can then be shed, but that the rest of the garment can breathe.

Perhaps the most popular shell garment for the upper body is made of nylon-cotton or polyester-cotton combinations, which breathe, are heavy but quite abrasion-resistant, and turn reasonable amounts of rain. The construction of such garments utilizes the ruggedness of the synthetic material in combination with the ability of cotton to swell and close its pores, thus shedding rain. Such garments are a compromise; they won't keep out rain as well as coated materials, but they're good in a variety of conditions. They do tend to freeze up badly if they get wet in winter weather.

All shell garments should be cut large enough to fit over all the insulation layers that may be worn underneath. Too often they aren't made roomy enough to fit over down or polyester parkas without compressing them and reducing their warmth. Large and baggy shell garments are generally best.

Waterproof shell clothing is essential for rainy conditions. Plastic rainwear can serve for emergency protection, but it's so fragile that it's uneconomical except in regions where it's rarely needed. It's also a poor choice on long trips, since, if it tears apart in the middle of a week of rain, the wearer is left with no protection. Mountaineers and others who may encounter severe wind-driven cold rain and sleet should never depend on light plastic raingear, which may be torn to shreds in the wind.

The standard material for lightweight raingear is coated

nylon material. If the seams are covered with some sealant such as Liquid Rubber, garments made of coated nylon do a good job of keeping rain out, but when you're working hard, the condensation of moisture from the body inside is often a major problem. On walking trips where wind isn't likely to be severe, the best solution is often a *poncho,* a large cape that has a hood in the middle and drapes loosely over the body. (Some designs cover the pack as well.) Rain is shed, but there's good ventilation to reduce condensation. The lightweight specialist may also use a large poncho as a shelter when camp is reached. Ponchos are most suitable for backpacking below timberline, since they afford little protection in high winds. Without sleeves, the canoeist is likely to have a lot of water running down her or his arms when a poncho is used for protection.

A garment similar to a poncho is made for cyclists, to fit over the upper body and the handlebars, but I've never found it terribly effective, because of the amount of spray that you frequently get from below. It's definitely useless on a bike without fenders. If you do use a cyclist's rain cape of this design, practice with it a little before you need it. The perspective with which the rider views the surroundings is changed quite a bit

Figure 7 Gaiters serve to keep snow and debris out of the boots as well as helping keep the lower legs warm, and they are useful on many trips. There are short models, but long ones like these are more suitable when deep snow may be encountered.

by the cape covering the view of the road behind the handlebars.

The alternatives to the poncho are full rainsuits of one
sort or another. These protect better against windblown rain
and are more suitable for activities requiring arm movement,
but condensation problems are greater. The most common arrangement is a rain parka and pants. A long, baggy parka called
a cagoule is preferred by many. With either a poncho or a
cagoule, chaps that cover the legs only are usually sufficient for
the lower part of the body. They're lighter and cheaper than
full rain pants.

BASIC CLOTHES

Shirts, trousers, and such should be tough and should not con-
strict movement. People's preferences vary, and materials are
not critical except when the weather is cold, wet, or both. In
these circumstances, wool or synthetic pile is by far the most
comfortable material, while cotton is the least. For most outdoor uses, at least some wool clothing is nice to have, in case
the weather turns bad. Most people get by with one long pair
of pants, a pair of shorts if balmy temperatures are expected,
a light shirt, such as an old cotton dress shirt or a T-shirt, a
wool shirt, and a sweater, together with shell clothing and
a light down or polyester vest or jacket for cool weather. For
cold weather or chilly water trips, long wool underwear can
be added, while the light pants are switched for a heavy wool
pair, and the shorts and light shirt are traded for an extra
wool shirt or sweater.

Always carry a warm hat for cool weather. The head is
amply supplied with blood at all times, and in cold weather
it can radiate a tremendous amount of heat. A wool stocking
cap or balaclava (a hat with an extension that can be pulled

down over the neck, ears, and back of the head) is one of the
most effective and lightest forms of insulation.

INSULATING CLOTHING

Warm shirts and sweaters make perfectly adequate clothing for
nearly any situation, provided enough are carried. Most campers like to take a warm vest or parka insulated with lightweight
and compressible down or polyester batting, however. Such garments can provide welcome extra insulation in the event of an
unexpected cold snap or lend a little extra warmth in the
sleeping bag at night. They are always pleasant luxury items
around camp in the evening and can be very useful during
lunch stops in winter. They also have the important advantages
of being light and easily stuffed into a small corner of the pack.

Down is superior for providing the maximum amount of
insulation for a given weight and packed size. This advantage
is less apparent in garments than in sleeping bags, however,
because clothing has to be overstuffed somewhat with down, to
prevent compression when the wearer moves around. Clothing
is also likely to get damp in many situations, either because of
precipitation or perspiration, and the polyester insulators are
much more effective when damp than down is. Polyester retains
most of its loft (thickness) when wet, and it dries quickly; down
is very poor in both respects.

Those buying puffy vests or jackets should thus consider
their needs carefully. If you're looking for a garment that's
primarily an emergency item, not to be used much, and therefore preferably as light and compact as possible, down is
probably the best alternative, provided the emergency you're
preparing for doesn't involve a lot of rain and wet weather.
Similarly, a touch of sumptuous warmth for the evening may
be best provided by a down jacket. If you plan to wear the

clothing when you're slogging up a hill, though, or if you may use it in sleet, along a river, or under raingear, you're better off with one of the polyester garments. The latter are also invariably cheaper than good down ones. More information on down and polyester insulation is included in the chapter on sleeping bags.

HOT WEATHER CLOTHES

When the weather is balmy and the sun isn't too much for your skin, it's pleasant to wear shorts and a T-shirt—or even more abbreviated clothing. Be careful of excessive exposure to sun, however, especially in the desert, in the high mountains, on water, or where there's a lot of snow. Sunburn on wilderness trips can be a serious matter. In conditions with a lot of sun and glare, long, loose-fitting cotton clothing is best.

Always carry a sun hat for hot weather. A light-colored cotton hat with a brim wide enough to give your eyes and neck some protection is best. Cheap cotton hats sold for tennis are fine. Sunglasses are a necessity in bright conditions. Snow blindness can occur as a result of glare off water or sand as well as snow, and it's incapacitating for several days.

SPECIALIZED CLOTHING

Long-distance cyclists generally wear close-fitting shorts of stretchy material that have crotches lined with chamois, to minimize chafing. Less essential are special cycling shirts which cut the wind well, fit closely to minimize flapping, and have pockets in the back where they are most useful for bicycle

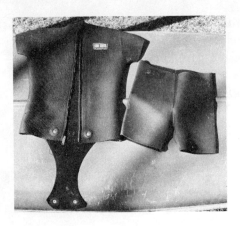

Figure 8 Paddlers who may be dumped into cold water wear wet suits of neoprene foam for safety. A short suit like this is for moderate conditions; a full-length suit is necessary for very cold water.

riders. When the weather is chilly, the cyclist can pull on special arm and leg warmers or wear an athletic warm-up suit over regular cycling clothes. Cyclists in warm weather generally wear fingerless gloves with padded palms. These reduce the pressure of handlebars against the nerves of the hand and provide some protection in case of a spill.

Water trippers active in chilly weather or far out on cold water need to wear *wet suits* for protection from the cooling effects of water. Suits made of ⅛-inch-thick neoprene material are the norm. A shirt alone or a short suit worn under wool clothing is adequate with reasonable air temperatures and water not much below 50° F (10° C). In colder conditions a full suit or a combination that overlaps at the midriff is desirable. Wet suits are available from white-water shops or diving stores. They can also be made at home using a kit or sheet neoprene material.

Many white-water boaters use a special shell top called a *paddling jacket,* made of coated material with tight closures at the wrists and neck to keep water from circulating easily. Depending on temperatures, a paddling jacket may be worn alone, over wool clothing, or over a wet suit. It greatly reduces the chilling effects of both wind and water.

chapter 4 | **Footgear**

Footgear is important for a lot of outdoor activities, and it deserves serious attention for several reasons. The most important is that on long trips sore and blistered feet can ruin the experience you'd planned to enjoy. A lot of boots and specialized shoes are also rather costly, so that badly chosen boots may prove to be an expensive mistake.

As with most equipment choices, thinking about what you expect to do is the most important phase of the purchase. A few activities require specialized footwear. Long-distance bicycle tours are easier with cyling shoes. Kayakers need lightweight shoes that can be used for wading and swimming. Climbers on different technical routes need specialized boots or shoes. For most outdoor activities, however, good hiking boots will do very nicely, and they make excellent auxiliary shoes for boating and climbing as well. Since they're the most versatile footwear, they'll be considered first.

HIKING BOOTS

Starting off with the "don'ts" may be appropriate in the case of boots, because so many people go out and buy the worst possible footwear for what they are going to do. Don't buy a pair of heavy technical *mountaineering boots*. Heavy mountaineering boots aren't designed for walking any more than high heels are. People who are going out to climb near-vertical ice need them, and they have to put up with the discomfort of wearing them while walking to and from their climbs. It's interesting that most people who wear mountaineering boots for climbing don't

Figure 9 Boots for wilderness wear have to be adaptable to a wide range of conditions, protecting the feet and giving good traction on all sorts of terrain. Sturdy hiking boots serve well in most situations.

wear them around town, on day hikes, or on easy backpacking trips. They tend to wear the lightest shoes that will serve their purpose. At least 95 percent of the people who buy boots of this kind need something a lot lighter and a lot cheaper.

Don't buy boots from your friendly discount store or fashion-shoe salon. You may find good boots there occasionally, but unless you know a lot about boot construction and leather, you'll probably get a lot less than your money's worth. If you can't afford decent hiking boots, make do with a pair of ankle-high work boots or tennis shoes; they're cheaper than poor-quality hiking boots, and they'll work just as well.

Don't buy boots when you're in a hurry. It takes time to find what you want, and it takes time to fit them properly. Old tennis shoes that fit are better than fine hiking boots that don't. If the salesperson is in a hurry, look elsewhere; hiking boots take patience to fit.

Finally, don't buy boots that are too tight. Your feet will swell when you're hiking, unless you do it every day. The increased blood supply to working feet increases their size quite a lot, and if the boots barely fit when you have only walked back and forth across the store a few times, they will be excruciatingly tight after several miles on the trail.

The function of *hiking boots* is to protect the feet from the roughness of the trail and to keep out water, snow, mud, stones, and the like as much as possible. Universal prescriptions are impossible, since people's feet and their needs vary a lot. It is, after all, possible to toughen the feet sufficiently to permit comfortable carrying of heavy loads on rough trails with bare feet. For the great majority, however, a good compromise has proved to be a pair of reasonably sturdy but lightweight shoes that come to about ankle height. They should have lug soles for good traction and should be flexible enough after breaking in to permit comfortable walking, the boots flexing at the balls of the feet, where feet are meant to flex. Except in the driest climates, they should be made of full-grain leather, which breathes but can be made reasonably watertight when that is

desirable. Boots higher than the ankle add a lot of weight with
little additional protection, and they tend to form creases at the
rear of the ankle, which then irritate the sensitive Achilles
tendons. If you plan to wade around in water above the ankles,
no leather boot will keep your feet dry. Truly waterproof boots
are good only for very specialized purposes; the feet sweating
inside get wet anyway and tend to become soft and easily
blistered.

FITTING BOOTS

Many beginners tend to worry a lot about the construction of
boots and very little about the way they fit. The priorities
should be reversed. Even a poorly made pair of hiking boots
that falls apart after the first year of use is a better buy than a
pair that lasts forever but fits so badly that your feet hurt all
the time you're wearing them. Most people don't walk very
much any more, and they're used to buying shoes that have to
get them only around the house or to the car. Long walks on
rough ground are much more demanding, particularly when
a heavy pack is carried. Perfectly fitting boots are particularly
important if your feet aren't toughened by frequent walking or
running.

Buy your socks first, so that you can accurately try boots
on over them, and be sure to take them with you when you go
out to try on boots. It's difficult enough to fit a pair of boots
without having to estimate the effect of a different thickness of
socks.

Boots that fit properly should feel comfortable and roomy,
but not allow your feet to slide around a lot. The heel should
be fairly snug, but the toes should have plenty of room. Walk
around the store for a while, and give irritation points a chance
to make themselves felt. Try to force your feet forward in the

boots, preferably by standing on a steeply sloping surface. If your toes hit the fronts of the boots easily, the boots are too short. Long downhill trails can be very painful when the toes are hitting at every step. Remember that your feet will swell, so the toes will hit more easily on the trail than in the shop. Walk around the store for an hour or two, if necessary, to be sure of the fit. Unless you're used to wearing boots, they'll feel strange at first, but they shouldn't rub, chafe, or irritate anywhere. If they rub in such a short time, they'll be far worse after many hours on the trail with a pack.

Boots are naturally a little stiff until they're broken in, but the sole should bend where your foot does and not remain so rigid that you can't walk naturally. Long steel shanks are common in heavy mountaineering boots, to prevent the boot from bending when the climber stands on his toes on small holds or crampon points. Just the opposite action is desirable for walking, where easy flexing at the ball of the foot is important.

Make sure that boots can be returned if you get them home and find that they don't fit after all. Wear them around for a while inside the house before taking them outside and committing yourself to them irretrievably.

BOOT CONSTRUCTION

The uppers of all satisfactory boots are still made from leather; no synthetic substitute has been found that works nearly so well. The hide from which a piece of leather is cut has a smooth side, called the grain, where the hair of the animal grew, and a rough side, called the flesh. Leather for boots should be taken from the tougher parts of the hide. The leather from around the belly, for example, is much weaker and thinner than that from the rump. A hide is often split into more than one layer, resulting in a thin piece with the grain on one side, which may be used for wallets, purses, and similar items, and one or more *splits,* which are rough on both sides. Suede comes from such splits, and it is often used for rock-climbing shoes and less expensive hiking boots. Good-quality splits are quite resistant to abrasion, and boots made from them are fine for dry weather, but it's impossible to make them water-repellent, because the flesh side of the leather is too porous to hold waxes and oils.

Boots that are expected to be reasonably watertight must be made with full-grain leather, that is, the smooth side must still be on the leather. Though far denser and more water-resistant than the flesh, the grain is very easily abraded. If a boot is made with the grain side facing out, rough use will cut, tear, and shred most of the grain, so that the boot loses its repellency along with a significant part of the leather. It's far better for the flesh side of the leather to face out, so that the grain is on the inside of the boot, where it's protected from abrasion by the rough side of the leather. Properly designed hiking boots using full-grain leather thus look much the same as those using splits, because the rough side of the leather is on the outside of the boot in both cases. The distinction between the types is important, however. If you plan to use your boots in wet conditions, be sure that they're made with full-grain but with the rough side facing out.

Boots should be made with as few seams on the outside of the upper as possible. Be particularly wary of uppers that are joined by a seam running down one side or the other of the boot: They tend to wear badly. Large amounts of padding inside a boot are unnecessary and undesirable. Sponge rubber is used for such padding, and boots incorporating it dry slowly. The illusion of insulation provided by the padding is false; the spongy stuff extends only through the ankle area.

Boots are so expensive that they should be durable enough to last through several pairs of soles. This means that the soles have to be replaceable. One-piece injection-molded soles bonded directly to the leather can't be replaced, and using them is generally a poor way to construct hiking boots. It's also impos-

Figure 10 Both these boots are made with full-grain leather with the rough side out, so that they can be rendered water-resistant. They're both lined with a lighter leather. The boot on the right is a heavy, stiff mountaineering boot, good for snow and ice climbing, but not very comfortable for walking. The one on the left is lighter, more flexible, and far more suitable for general hiking, backpacking, and normal outdoor use. The construction of the two boots also differs. The one on the left is stitched on the inside, whereas the other is made with a Norwegian welt and has two rows of outside stitching showing along the top of the sole. The tongues of both boots are gusseted and well sealed against the entry of water and debris.

sible for a shoe repairman to fix injection-molded boots if the uppers begin to pull away from the soles. So if you buy boots of this type, find out what guarantee the shop will give you.

There are several other ways to fasten soles to hiking-boot uppers, and they're chosen primarily to suit the construction equipment of the manufacturer. The least suitable is called a *Goodyear welt,* employing a narrow strip of leather to which the insole, midsole, and upper are sewn. The lug sole is then glued to the midsole. The Goodyear welt requires outside stitching that penetrates into the interior of the boot, providing a route for water to leak in. If the narrow welt is damaged by rough wear, it may not be repairable.

The most common construction for heavy mountaineering boots and for many lighter ones is called a *Norwegian welt*. It has two rows of outside stitching, like the Goodyear welt. The edge of the upper is first sewn directly to the insole and then to the midsole. An extra strip of leather may be added around the stitching lines, called a storm welt. This construction is stronger than the Goodyear welt, though it still allows water an easy entrance through the seam holes to the inside of the boot. The stitches are also in a position that subjects them to wear, but rarely to the point where they can't be repaired, except when they're used for a lot of rock climbing.

The best construction method for hiking boots is *inside stitching*, by which the upper is folded between the inner sole and the midsole and then stitched directly through, with the lug sole covering the outside of the stitches. This method of construction protects the stitches from abrasion, allows the sole to be trimmed even with the upper, and leaves no passage for water into the boot.

The recommendations on construction mentioned here are general ones, and the buyer should take some time to look at boots available in different shops. Remember that the most important consideration in buying boots is fit. Durability, reasonably light weight, and special features are secondary.

A fairly simple shoe is usually best. Gusseting around the tongue or covering flaps are useful in keeping out water and stones, but most other extras are of little importance. Padded collars at the top of a boot tend to wear and rot easily, since they're normally made of a thin glove leather. If padding is used there, it's best attached inside the rim of heavy leather, rather than in a little ring—or, worse yet, several of them— above the durable leather. Hinges at the back of the ankle are generally a bad idea, since they fall apart long before the rest of the boot. Except for lightweight split-leather shoes, hiking boots are usually lined with a glove leather for smoothness, but this shouldn't be a criterion for judging quality. All sorts of hardware for lacing are touted for different reasons; one type works as well as another.

BOATING SHOES

Various kinds of footwear have been tried for canoeing, kayaking, rafting, and other water travel, some successfully and some not. It's best to decide at the start whether you're likely to keep your feet dry or whether they'll inevitably get wet. In canoeing on calm water where the landing spots are solid, you may well be able to maintain dry feet most of the time, despite an occasional mishap. For this sort of boating, I prefer to wear hiking boots, which give good footing on steep banks and tricky portage trails. Others use work shoes, which are lighter, more flexible, and faster-drying. Still others like rubber-bottom boots, particularly when the weather is cool, because they permit stepping in several inches of water or wading occasional marshy spots without wetting the feet. On the other hand, perspiration condensing inside rubber-bottom boots is a problem.

Those using one of these types of footwear usually also carry some kind of lightweight shoes, for wearing around camp, wearing during a long day of paddling down a big lake, or changing into when the other shoes have gotten wet. Moccasins, sneakers, and running shoes are common choices for auxiliary footwear.

Wet feet are an unavoidable feature of many water trips, and trying to keep shoes dry in these situations is a waste of time and energy. The simplest solution is a pair of high-top sneakers. Old worn-out ones with lots of holes through which the water can drain are a favorite. Wool socks are worn inside if the weather isn't too cool. On colder trips, larger sneakers

Figure 11 Specialized footwear is often necessary for particular purposes, especially boating, skiing, cycling, and technical climbing. These rubber-bottom boots are preferred by many canoeists in cool weather where a lot of soggy ground may be encountered. They are also good for hiking or flat, marshy terrain.

can be worn, leaving space inside for a pair of socks made of neoprene wet-suit material. With such footwear, you can simply step into the water when necessary, rather than prancing around in a futile effort to keep the feet dry by walking on slippery rocks. Shoes should be worn even in warm weather, because of the danger of sharp rocks or broken bottles on the bottom. With neoprene socks, the feet stay warm even if the water is very cold. A second pair of shoes is also carried by wet-shoe theorists, to change into at the end of the day, wear on long portages, or hike up nearby hills or side canyons. A pair of hiking boots serves the purpose well.

CYCLING SHOES

For short bicycle trips, just about any shoes will do, from sneakers to hiking boots, but on longer rides there is a definite advantage to having special cycling shoes. Ideally these should be lightweight and well ventilated except in cold weather. The soles should be fairly stiff, particularly at the front where the foot rests on the edges of the pedal. They should either incorporate cleats that grip the pedals positively or be thick enough to allow them to be installed. Cleats are grooved pieces, usually made of metal, which lock onto the rear edges of pedals when toe straps are pulled tight. Good cycling shoes with cleats permit far more efficient pedaling because the legs can pull as well as push on the pedals and because the feet remain exactly in place on the pedals.

Ventilation is important with cycling shoes, because the feet bend less than they do when walking and are usually pulled down tight against the pedals by straps. Sweating and circulation problems tend to be common, particularly around the ball of the foot. Holes through the sole of the shoe help somewhat, provided they're large enough to provide real ventilation. The thickness and stiffness of the sole are partly a matter of personal preference, but good protection from the pedals is usually welcomed by novices on their first long trip.

Lightweight, coated nylon booties over the shoes are helpful in cutting the wind and water in cold or rainy weather. Holes can be cut for the cleats, though if the material isn't too thick, the cleats often grip well anyway. If the weather is really cold, old wool socks a couple of sizes larger than normal will go over cycling shoes, with holes cut for the cleats and booties worn over the socks to cut the wind. For warmth, an alternative is a pair of light overboots designed to go over ski-touring boots.

Cycling shoes are not very convenient around camp or in buildings. The problem of clicking metal cleats can be solved by getting a pair of leather cleats, which are sold by the Touring Cyclist. Most campers put up with the extra weight of a pair of light running shoes or something similar to change into.

SKI-TOURING BOOTS

Ski-touring boots are usually fairly specialized, made to fit into pin bindings that clamp to the toes of the boots. The most common type is a lightweight boot of ankle height or lower with a flexible injection-molded sole. A plate with three holes is normally installed in the toe of the sole, which mates with the three pins that project from Nordic bindings. Pin bindings give good skiing control, and they're lightweight, simple, and relatively trouble-free, making them quite suitable for most backcountry touring.

The standard types of touring boots themselves aren't very suitable for overnight trips, because they're quite light and provide little protection for the feet after skis are removed. Even when a skier using them has stopped, the lack of movement slows circulation in the feet. Several alternatives are preferred by different winter campers. Some use somewhat heavier boots, which may include a little insulation; while these may be suited to backcountry use, they're usually still too light to give good protection around camp. One alternative is to carry overboots which can be worn around camp over the boots or over insulated down or synthetic booties. One of the best solutions is to use foam-insulated *overboots* which fit over standard Nordic boots and can be worn all the time when the weather is cold or in camp when needed. They can be made to fit any of the standard Nordic bindings. For those who have great problems with cold feet, are interested in ski mountaineering with touring equipment, or have other special needs, there are double ski-touring boots with lug soles made by Galibier, which are flexible enough for use with normal Nordic equipment and techniques. These boots are available from Steve Komito, Bootmaker, P.O. Box 2106, Estes Park, Colorado 80517.

CLIMBING BOOTS AND SHOES

There are a number of highly specialized types of footwear designed for rock climbing and mountaineering. Normal hiking boots are quite suitable for moderate climbing and a lot of general mountaineering. Rock climbers often use special lightweight shoes both for the increased control they afford and because they may be cheaper than heavier boots. Rock climbing shoes are usually fitted tightly, however, and they're very uncomfortable to wear for hiking any distance. Heavy mountaineering boots have been mentioned earlier in connection with hiking. The stiff shanks used in the soles of mountaineering boots serve to relieve the calf muscles of the climber kicking steps in snow or using crampons (frames with spikes that fit on the bottoms of the boots) for climbing ice. On difficult mountaineering routes, such boots are often necessary, and they serve the climber well enough for the hikes to and from climbs, once his or her feet have been accustomed to them. For winter and expeditionary climbing, there are special double boots and various types of overboots available.

SOCKS

Socks can be even more important than boots in keeping the feet warm, comfortable, and free from blisters, Buy your socks first, so that you can fit boots over them. Many sock combinations and materials have been tried over the years. The vast majority of outdoors people have found the most satisfactory combination to be a heavy pair of wool ragg socks (a traditional Norwegian type, knitted with coarse, undyed wool) over a lighter pair of soft-wool, bulked-Orlon, silk, or olefin inner socks. The inner socks protect all but the most sensitive skin from irritation by the rough wool of the ragg socks.

This fairly heavy sock combination helps keep the feet warm in cold weather, provides a good deal of cushioning and protection from the unaccustomed hard use the feet receive in backcountry travel, and wicks moisture away from the feet so they don't become too tender. The double layer is useful in reducing the friction that causes blisters, and it's preferable in hot weather as well as cold.

Carrying several pairs of socks is worthwhile, particularly for beginning hikers and backpackers with tender, citified feet. Changing to dry socks during the day can reduce friction and help keep the feet dry and relatively tough. Spare pairs can be washed in dry weather and dried on the pack while under way. Dirty socks increase friction, and salts from perspiration tend to retain moisture.

Neoprene socks for use in cold water have already been mentioned. Cyclists generally use lighter socks than other lightweight travelers, although preferences vary a good deal, ranging from bare feet inside cycling shoes to heavy socks.

| chapter | **Sleeping Bags** |
| 5 | **And Mats** |

A sleeping bag is generally the most expensive piece of equipment that the lightweight camper needs to buy, and a good one will last a long time with proper care. The bag is an important investment in comfort and pleasure as well, because it can frequently make the difference between an enjoyable trip and a miserable one. For most people, particularly those who don't fancy themselves to be tough as nails, the difference between a good night's sleep and a poor one is also the difference between a pleasant trip and a rotten one. A warm, comfortable bed can soothe away a lot of hard traveling, but a sleepless night can ruin even the best of days. It's possible to accustom yourself to sleeping in rough conditions, but the beginner used to civilized living is likely to have a lot more fun if she or he doesn't try to get by with Spartan sleeping gear.

With sleeping bags more than with any other item, it's unwise to cut corners in an attempt to save money. There are bargains in the secondhand market, clearance sales, and the like. Less expensive materials or methods of construction may suit your needs, but discount operations offering wonderful deals generally also offer shoddy merchandise. A good *down bag* that's well cared for should last most campers more than a decade, but cheap materials and poor construction often shorten that time to a year. For a given type of bag, only a little money can be saved by the maker by using less expensive materials; most savings can be made only in labor costs, and poorly made bags are the usual result. A seamstress can do a seam twice as fast by using half as many stitches per inch, but the resulting sleeping bag will wear out twice as fast.

ANALYZING YOUR NEEDS

Before you buy a sleeping bag, it's very important to consider the requirements of your own body as well as the conditions you expect to encounter. The temperature ratings mentioned by manufacturers are of very little value except as a basis for comparing bags made by the same company. Sleeping bags are used for a multitude of purposes, ranging from sleeping in a lean-to shelter along the Appalachian Trail in the summer to living at high altitudes on mountains in the winter. A bag can't be suitable for sleeping both at 60° F (16° C) and at −40° F (−40° C). Individual variations are almost as great. Some people tend to be quite warm when they sleep, even with little covering, in cool temperatures. Others sleep cold and require a lot of insulation for comfort when the nights are mild. Before you begin to decide what sort of bag you need, it's important to consider both what kind of camping you intend to do and where you fit on the spectrum of individual needs for insulation while sleeping.

To give an example of the extremes that are possible, I've slept quite comfortably in subfreezing weather in a 1½-pound down bag with sewn-through seams, while a good friend of mine wisely purchased a six-pound expedition down bag, though she rarely encounters temperatures below freezing. Either of these choices would be unusual, but they illustrate the variation in individual needs. A person who's generally colder than others and who needs more blankets or sleeps in a warmer room than others needs a bag considerably warmer than average for particular circumstances. A person who sleeps warmer than average, is conditioned to the cold and is in good physical shape, or is experienced in the techniques for staying warm at night may be able to get by with a lighter bag.

The conditions in which the bag will be used are probably the most important consideration for most people. What is the normal temperature range in which the bag will be used? What extremes should it be suitable for? Will it be easy to keep the bag dry, or will wet conditions make this difficult? Windy sleeping conditons, sleeping under the sky, sleeping on snow, and fatigue all have an effect similar to low temperatures, and they should be considered as well.

A good basis for comparison in analyzing your requirements is the *three-season bag* that has evolved over the years as the most popular sleeping bag produced by experienced suppliers of good backpacking equipment. Such a bag may not be the best compromise for you, but it has proved its versatility and usefulness for many people, so it's the perfect bag with which to begin our discussion. It has a modified mummy shape, tapered like the body, so as to give efficient insulation with a minimum of weight, but cut so that it's sufficiently roomy to allow the sleeper to move around a little inside the bag. It's normally made of thin, tightly woven nylon material, which is strong, light, and is smooth enough not to bind a sleeper easily. The insulation is traditionally down, the undercoat of waterfowl, an expensive material that's difficult to work with. High quality down, despite the attempts of technology to improve upon it, provides more insulation for a given weight, can be compressed into a smaller space, and continues to spring back for more years than any substitute.

A typical three-season bag of good quality will keep the average person comfortable in a sheltered spot, such as a tent, down to a temperature of perhaps 10° F (−12° C), with a good

Figure 12 Sleeping bags may be designed for widely varying conditions, and it's important to analyze your own needs carefully before looking at them. A bag designed for winter conditions at high altitude, like those in this windy spot, is different from one made for a milder climate. An igloo is visible in the center of the picture; such snow shelters are ideal for winter camping.

ground bed. The range can be extended by wearing clothing inside the bag, using a sleeping bag cover, and so forth. The same person will probably find the bag fairly comfortable up to a temperature of 60° F (16° C) or so before needing a lot of ventilation. Such bags commonly have full-length side zippers which open from both the bottom and the top for ventilation. This sort of bag is a good choice on backpacking trips in the western mountains for a person who has average insulation requirements. It makes a useful starting point to judge one's own needs. People who sleep cold will need to add insulation for restful sleep, while those camping mainly in the summer at lower elevations will be more comfortable with more lightly insulated bags which weigh less, are more compact, and prevent the occupants from sweating on most nights. An individual who plans on extensive cold-weather camping in severe conditions may want a warmer bag, but by adding clothing and using other methods, a standard three-season bag can usually be made to serve very well for snow camping.

Other needs should be considered before going out to choose a bag. If price is an important consideration, it may be worthwhile to sacrifice some of the weight and bulk advantages of the down bag and choose one using synthetic insulation instead. There are good backpacking bags made now using polyester insulators. In fact, if you expect to camp a lot in wet conditions, there are good arguments for using synthetic bags, which are far less vulnerable to moisture than down. Try to get a good idea of your own needs before starting to look at the sleeping bags themselves. You'll see all kinds of pleasing features with lots of appeal, but many of them are designed for someone else's needs rather than yours. If what you need is a bag that's warm down to about the freezing point, then one that's cozy at −40° F (−40° C) is a waste of money, and it's also far heavier and bulkier than necessary. Get a precise idea of your requirements first, then look at the market to find a bag that meets them.

SLEEPING BAG DESIGN

As with clothing, the fundamental principle in sleeping bag design is that warmth is directly proportional to thickness. The statement needs some qualification, but not as much as with clothing, because the function of a sleeping bag is almost completely one of insulation. Far less consideration needs to be given to abrasion resistance, weather resistance, and the like. The sleeping bag is normally used in a protected spot, with minimal body movement. Since the bag must be carried while it's not in use, minimal weight and packed bulk are desirable, consistent with reasonable comfort in sleeping. Thus, the huge, heavy, inefficient bags normally sold for car camping are generally shunned by the lightweight camper, though minimal weight and tight packing are more important in some forms of self-propelled camping than others. The cyclist and the mountaineer are likely to be the most demanding, and the canoeist the least.

Insulation does not provide any warmth itself; its purpose is to slow the many kinds of energy transfer that dissipate the body's heat. If more heat escapes than is produced, the body will begin to cool, and the sleeper is likely to wake up tense and shivering, as the body is forced to increase its heat output. Far more insulation is needed at night than is required at similar temperatures during the day, because heat production is lower when one is asleep. Variations in resting heat production, sensitivity to cold, and natural insulation of the body account for the great differences in the need for insulation. People who are tired also produce less heat at rest. There are many other physical variations, some of which can be controlled and will be discussed in Chapter IX.

Heat can be conducted away from the body in a number of ways. Direct conduction to the cold ground is an important one, and it is controlled mainly by a sleeping pad, which is discussed later in this chapter. Radiation to cold surroundings, particularly a clear sky, can be significant, but it can be largely controlled with proper camping technique. This is the type of loss that is reduced by the use of many much-touted "space-age materials" like reflective aluminum. If you plan on camping a lot in outer space, floating about in the void, this is the proper sort of insulation. If, however, you'll be doing your camping on earth, convection by cold air is the problem, and wrapping oneself in a thin reflective layer won't solve it. Convective transfer occurs when cold air molecules strike your skin or a surface warmed by your skin and bounce off, carrying some of your body's heat away with them. The process is accelerated greatly if the air is moving so that fresh cold air is always being circulated past the body. That's why the wind-chill factor operates to make the effect of an increase in wind speed similar to an actual drop in temperature.

In most practical situations, the best insulator available is air, provided it can be kept in many small compartments with little movement between. This is particularly true for the lightweight traveler, because air can be found and appropriated anywhere. All one has to carry is a cocoon of compartments that can be stuffed into the pack when it's not needed, but will expand when removed from the pack, filling up with air that's held still in a lot of little chambers. Virtually all insulators used in clothing, sleeping bags, and houses are really just that: honeycomb-like structures designed to hold a still layer of air between a warm interior and a cold exterior. The insulating value depends only on how still the air layer really is and how thick it is. Because of this, an inch-thick layer of polyester insulation maintains just about the same warmth as an inch-thick layer of down, fiberglass mat, wool, cotton batting, or shredded newspaper. Other factors give one or another the advantage, but the insulation value is the same.

The other factors are important to the self-propelled camper. Ideally the insulating material should weigh next to nothing, should hold the layer of air it absorbs absolutely still, and should be easy to form into a sleeping bag. Moreover, it should compress into a tiny package yet bounce back as soon as it is released and as often as the bag is used, should be unaffected by moisture, dirt, or perspiration, and should be cheap. The materials which some closest to meeting these requirements are waterfowl down and synthetic polyester batting. For a given amount of insulation, the down is lighter, compresses into a smaller package, continues to bounce back for a much longer time, and is generally comfortable over a wider temperature range. The polyesters are initially cheaper, simpler to handle in bag manufacture, and easier to clean; their insulating value is affected much less and for a much shorter time by moisture than down. Finally, the quality of a given type of polyester is uniform, whereas down quality is quite variable.

Other factors besides insulating material radically affect the warmth of a sleeping bag. If a bag fits close to the body, there's less air inside the bag to circulate and cool the sleeper, and the outside surface area is smaller, so it loses less heat to the environment. Such a close-fitting bag can also be made thicker and therefore warmer while using less material. Close-fitting bags are warmer and lighter than loose-fitting ones, provided they're properly designed, but some people can sleep comfortably in much narrower bags than others. Almost anyone can learn to be happy with a modified mummy design. The big rectangular bags may seem more accommodating at first, because they're more like a bed at home, but carrying one up a trail is a lot like hauling an old four-poster. A modified mummy design, with a girth at the shoulders of around 60 to 64 inches, is roomy enough to allow you to move around quite a bit inside the bag and is fairly easy for most people to get used to. Tighter bags make many campers feel rather constrained and claustrophobic, but even this feeling can be overcome by getting used to moving with the bag rather than inside it.

Whether or not the savings in weight justify a tighter bag is a personal choice, but the weight savings can be considerable. There's normally a difference in weight of about one pound between a standard modified mummy-style bag and a lightweight bag cut fairly closely that are made by the same manufacturer and rated at the same level of warmth. The difference is even greater in bags insulated with synthetic materials.

Several other important design features are common to all kinds of bags. Except in limited-purpose bags where every possible ounce is to be saved, there should be a zipper running at least three-quarters of the length of the bag, preferably full-length with a slider at the bottom as well as the top for ventilation. Ventilation is the biggest advantage conferred by the zipper, since it makes a bag usable over a much wider range

Figure 13 Desert conditions illustrate the contrasting requirements that the wilderness traveler may have. Temperatures in the desert can vary widely, particularly in the spring and fall; in March, evening figures can range between −10° and 55° F (−23° C and 12° C).

of temperatures. Bags from the same manufacturer with zippers on opposite sides can usually be zipped together, a companionable feature, but one that doesn't contribute significantly to the warmth of the occupants since the resulting double bag is much too well ventilated. Either the zipper should be backed up with an insulated draft tube or there should be two zippers, one attached to the inside shell and one to the outside. In either case, the function is to prevent the zipper from being a cold seam.

The hood and the neck of the bag should be designed so they can be easily adjusted, usually by a drawstring clamp on the opposite side from the zipper. It should be possible to pull the hood tight around the head and face without squashing the insulation. Insulation around the head and neck is particularly important on cold nights: The blood supply to these areas is excellent, so they can dissipate body warmth very quickly.

Drafts entering around the face can also chill the whole inside of the bag.

Both the thickness of the insulating layer and its uniformity affect the warmth of the bag. Warm weather sleeping bags are often made with a quilted construction of some kind, the insulation simply being sewn into compartments made by stitching the outside fabric of the bag to the inside. This method is inexpensive and fairly effective, but the cold seams make it inappropriate for constructing bags designed for cooler temperatures. In warmer bags, more sophisticated construction methods must be used to leave no cold seams. Ideally the construction should result in a uniform layer of insulation that is held in place to prevent shifting. Shifting insulation results in thin, cold areas in the bag.

DOWN BAGS

Despite the immense improvements in synthetic insulation during the last few years and a decline in the quality of available down, a down bag can still be made that is as warm as a synthetic one weighing half again as much and having a good deal more bulk. The down bag will probably cost 50 percent more, but it will last more than twice as long. There are clearly still major advantages to down for the serious lightweight camper, provided he or she can keep the down dry.

Since down is composed of many little particles of fluff, unattached to one another, any sleeping bag containing it must be constructed so that the down is held in a large number of separate compartments. Otherwise the down tends to shift into corners of the bag, leaving the rest with no loft at all. (The *loft* is the thickness of the bag, the most important factor affecting warmth.) In general, the smaller the compartments, the more control over down shift is gained and the more uniform loft is achieved with a given amount of down. (Alternatively, larger compartments can be stuffed with more down.) However, more compartments require more fabric and more labor. The task of the bag designer is to achieve the optimum balance between these factors. The beginner should at least realize that the weight of filling is meaningless unless one knows the other features of a bag's construction as well. Stuffing more down, especially inferior quality down, into a bag is often much cheaper than building a more sophisticated bag. Though material costs are high in bag manufacture, labor costs are higher still.

Bags designed for cooler temperatures use a baffling system between the inside and outside fabric to form compartments for the down. The most common types of baffling are shown in Figure 14. The tubes formed by the baffling generally run across the bag, forming circumferential channels. These channels are often blocked by an additional baffle opposite the zipper, separating the bottom channels from the top ones. The material used for the baffling is much lighter than the shell material, usually either a stretchy net or a very lightweight ripstop nylon. The loft of the bag is determined both by the

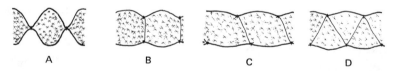

A   B   C   D

Figure 14 Some common construction methods for down sleeping bags in cross section. (a) Sewn-through construction. The outer and inner shells are stitched together to form tubes that hold the down filling, a construction suitable only for warm weather or inner bags, because the "cold seams" have no insulation. (b) Box or I-beam baffling. A series of walls made of lightweight material are sewn between the two shells to control the down. This baffle construction is much more difficult to produce, but far more efficient than sewn-through construction. (c) Slant-wall or parallelogram baffling. It has some advantages over the box baffling, but is also slightly heavier. (d) Triangular baffling. This method gives maximum control of the down filling and requires maximum labor and material. It is normally used only in bags designed for expedition conditions.

down filling and by the size of the channels when they're expanded by the down. Up to a point, weight can be reduced by sewing in channels closer together, so that the down is prevented from shifting. This raises the price of the bag a good deal because of the extra material and labor involved. There's also a limit to the productivity of the method, since adding more material eventually outweighs the down saved.

The baffling material, the down, and much of the workmanship are hidden from view in a completed bag, so the shopper has to rely on what he or she can see from the outside and on the reputation of the manufacturer. Weights are important, of course, and they're often different from those advertised, even in bags made by reputable suppliers. Consequently, it's worth checking the actual weight of a bag you're considering. The relative interior sizes of bags can either be measured or simply judged comparatively by how tightly they fit. Ask the salesman or check the catalog regarding the construction and advertised loft of the bag. A bag with the baffles placed four inches apart will allow much less down shift than one with six-inch spacing. Compress the sleeping bag into a stuff bag, and then after it has been stuffed for a while, pull it out and see how much fluffing is required to return it to full loft. Look through a single layer of the bag at a strong light after it's fluffed to determine whether there are thin spots. Feel for low insulation spots as well. After the bag has been fluffed, hold one side and shake the bag very gently to see if the down empties into one side. (Hard shaking will compress the down.) Significant shifting indicates that the down compartments are underfilled, and cold spots will be a problem.

Check the loft yourself with a ruler for comparison with other manufacturers' bags. Different makers measure loft in different ways, so that even when listed figures are honest, there may be considerable variation between companies' products.

Temperature ratings are useful for comparing bags within a particular line, but they're of little help in comparing the products of different makers. Similar bags are often rated for minimum temperatures 20 degrees apart by different manufacturers.

DOWN QUALITY

Since down is a natural product, its quality varies widely, depending on the nature of the birds from which it was plucked and on the handling of the down subsequently. A true down pod isn't a small feather; it's a complex of filaments radiating out from a central point without any quill. All so-called down used for insulation contains a number of small feathers, however, because there's no practical way to separate them during the plucking and processing of the down. Since the virtues of down sought by lightweight campers are maximum filling capacity for a minimum of weight and a resiliency that allows the down to pop back again and again for years, it's just these capacities which determine the quality of the down. Unfortunately, there's no very practical way for the buyer of a sleeping bag to determine the quality of down, except by the reputation of the manufacturer and external inspection of the finished bag.

The down which best meets the requirements is that with few feathers, minimum broken-fiber content, and a high proportion of large, fluffy pods of down. The best down comes from mature geese raised in a cold climate, and it retains its quality when it's properly washed, separated, and handled after the geese are plucked. Unfortunately, down of this type can't be found in commercial quantities. Most catalogs are designed to create an impression in the consumer's mind of some native craftsman carefully plucking down from a recently captured wild goose that has just flown down from Arctic latitudes. Dozens of different descriptive terms are used by manufacturers to describe this wondrous stuff, most of which mean absolutely nothing. Down is in fact one of the side products of the poultry industry, the main interest of which is meat. Waterfowl are raised and eaten only rarely in the United States, so most down originates in those parts of the world where geese and ducks are raised for the table. There's a large international market for down, and it's bought and sold through brokers. A down buyer for a sleeping bag manufacturer has no practical way of judging the origin of his down, except by looking at it and testing it. In general, the quality of down during the past decade or two has deteriorated, while the price has soared. This is true because demand has increased enormously, because the exchange rate of the dollar has declined, and because poultry raisers in many parts of the world have discovered, as American beef-raisers have, that the maximum number of pounds of meat can be produced at minimum cost by slaughtering animals young. The down from immature animals is not as fluffy or as resilient as that from older ones. Modern handling methods have offset some of this deterioration, but only to a degree. Down can be "fractionalized," to remove more feathers and smaller down pods, but the process is limited. All that can be done with this sort of process is to get some of the better down from the lot; there's no way to improve the filling power or toughness of individual down pods.

Legally, filling can be described as down when 80 percent of the material consists of down pods and fibers. Eighteen percent may be feathers and feather fragments, and the remainder may be dirt, iron filings, or anything else. Down can be legally described as goose down if 90 percent of the down content (72 percent of the total content) is down from geese. Though there are standardized methods of judging down quality, there are no legal descriptions. Descriptions in catalogs, such as "100% Prime Grade AAA Silverpuff Northern Goose Down" don't mean what you may think. You may think that the 100 percent refers to the goose down, but it doesn't; it refers to "Prime Grade AAA Silverpuff Northern," terms that are legally trade descriptions not subject to regulation. No filling standards are included; these are up to the manufacturer.

An individual bag manufacturer may have particular filling and feather-content standards, as well as requirements for cleanliness and the like, but these may or may not be specified in literature and catalogs. The most critical specification is filling power per ounce. Extremely high-quality down may have a filling power of 800 cubic inches per ounce. Most manufacturers of well-made lightweight equipment use down with a filling power of at least 550 cubic inches per ounce, but different grades are often used in different bags, and many makers don't specify their down standards.

All other things being equal, goose down is superior in filling power and durability to duck down because a goose-down cluster is more complex with a finer network of fibers than a duck-down cluster. All things may not be equal, however, and poor goose down is not nearly so suitable for making sleeping bags as good duck down, so a label stating that a product is filled with goose down does not necessarily mean it is better than one filled with duck down. Filling power and care in manufacture is more important than whether 80 percent of the down is from geese or ducks. It's worth mentioning that much imported duck down retains an unpleasant odor from the fish meal fed to the ducks. Smell the bag carefully, perhaps after wetting a small area, since the odor tends to come out with dampness and heat.

DIFFERENTIAL CUT

The simplest construction for a sleeping bag is to cut the inside and outside shells from the same pattern. In a baffled bag, the baffles are then sewn between the two shells. This method is quite suitable for bags made for mild temperatures, but there are several disadvantages for bags designed to be used in more extreme conditions. Since the insulation in lightweight bags is very compressible, the inside layer is easily pushed against the outside one when the elbows are pushed out or legs pulled up, making cold spots where the insulation is compressed. One way for a manufacturer to lessen this problem is to cut the lining of the bag smaller than the shell, so that even when a sleeper stretches the inside layer, it can't be pushed against the outer fabric. Because of the difference in circumference between the inner and the outer, this is known as a *differential cut*.

A differentially cut bag is harder to tailor and sew than one with identically cut liner and shell. The differential needs to be distributed properly to fit the body. A badly cut bag may tend to stand out from the body and be colder, but this isn't true of a properly cut bag.

There has been more heat than light generated over the years on the subject of a differential cut. With a large, roomy bag, a differential cut isn't essential, because the sleeper is less likely to press the liner out. Some excellent bags are made in modified mummy designs without a differential cut. The differential advantage is also less for people who move around less while sleeping. Thrashers and curlers are more likely to notice the virtues of the differential cut. Another advantage of the differential cut is the saving in weight. A few ounces may be shaved from a high-lofting bag because less material is used in the lining.

The importance of a differential cut will vary according to the camper and the bag being chosen. Any tightly fitting bag being purchased for cool weather should be differentially cut; close-fitting bags with the lining and shell cut to the same pattern develop cold spots every time the sleeper rolls over. People who move around a lot in their sleep will probably also be a little happier with a differential cut, though it isn't so critical in a roomier bag.

POLYESTER SLEEPING BAGS

Despite the major advantages of down mentioned above, those sleeping bags using polyester insulation have become good enough to replace down for many purposes. Most of these have been mentioned already and won't be repeated here. The greatest advantages of the polyesters, aside from price considerations, are their retention of some warmth when wet, their low moisture absorption, and the ease of drying them if they become wet. These characteristics make polyester bags very attractive for uses where moisture is a major problem: in very wet regions, on boating trips, in difficult mountaineering, and on many winter trips. The advantages are particularly great for beginners, who have often not learned all the tricks for keeping down dry, and for those who often camp in difficult situations where it's sometimes impossible to avoid wetting equipment.

The two main brands of polyester insulation in use at the time of this writing are DuPont's Dacron Fiberfill II and Celanese Fortrel PolarGuard. The two are roughly comparable in lofting capability and fiber structure. The main difference is that PolarGuard is made up of long continuous fibers, while Fiberfill is composed of many short fibers, a few inches long. Manufacturers of backpacking equipment are only beginning to learn to use the polyesters for lightweight equipment, and more effective designs may change the advantages of one fiber over another. But at the moment, PolarGuard seems to be superior for outdoor equipment, because the long fibers resist shifting and consequent lumping and development of cold spots in long-term use.

A number of manufacturers are now working with polyester insulation and making quality lightweight equipment, but there's still a tendency among many to view polyester bags as less worthy of careful design and manufacture than down bags. Fortunately, it's at least somewhat easier to judge quality in bags insulated with the synthetics, because the insulating material itself is of uniform and unvarying quality; the individual manufacturer can't have or claim to have some special source for a uniquely high-lofting variety of PolarGuard.

Some of the construction techniques used in making sleeping bags with polyester insulation are shown in Figure 15.

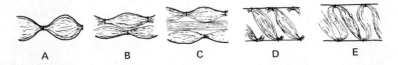

A   B   C   D   E

Figure 15 Some construction methods used in bags filled with synthetic material supplied in batts. (a) Sewn-through construction. As with down bags, this is the cheapest construction method, but one unsuited to bags made for cold-weather use. A similar construction that makes for a slightly warmer but perhaps less durable bag has the batting sewn to only one shell. (b) Offset construction. Two batts are used, one sewn to each shell, with the seams offset, so that cold spots don't coincide. (c) Three-layer construction, similar to offset, but with an extra batt between the other two. This center batt may be stabilized by being sewn in only at the edges or by being stitched to a very light layer of material. (d) Slant-wall construction using sections of batting sewn diagonally between the shells has been used successfully by North Face. (e) Another innovative construction method loops the batting back and forth between the shells.

Batts of the insulation material, sold in various weights per square yard, are normally sewn to a layer of nylon first, and then these nylon-batting quilts are used to construct the bag. When two layers of insulation are used, one batt is normally sewn to the lining material and one to the shell, and the two are put together in such a way as to offset the seams. If three layers of insulation are used, the middle layer must be reinforced in some way to stabilize it.

COMBINATIONS

There have been a number of recent attempts to combine the advantages of synthetics and down. For example, synthetics may be used on the ground side of a bag insulated on the opposite side with down. The polyester, which is less compressible than down, is thus placed where the body normally flattens down insulation. Foam pads, which are even less compressible than polyester, have also been incorporated in the bottoms of bags, but they pose some construction problems. A mixture of synthetic fibers and down called Fiberdown has been used by Gerry to insulate entire bags. It has a better loft for a given weight than synthetics, along with some of their drying advantages. It's used in loose fill construction, as down is.

One of the most interesting ways to combine the advantages of synthetics and down is with a *double-bag system,* using two separate sleeping bags, one of which is designed to fit inside the other. Such a system has the disadvantages of slightly heavier weight for a given amount of warmth, because the weight of an extra shell and lining must be included. However, the combination doesn't cost any more than a comparable winter-weight bag, it's far more versatile, and the purchase price can be split into two parts. The best double system uses a down inner bag, which should be cut fairly close, with a light synthetic outer bag. The down bag can be used alone on most trips where cool weather is expected, the synthetic outer bag can be used by itself on warm-weather trips, and both can be carried for cold weather and extreme conditions.

Versatility is a key advantage for a double system, particularly for the all-around lightweight camper, who wants to go bicycle touring one weekend, backpacking in the high country

Figure 16 A versatile double sleeping-bag system. In the foreground is a light Polarguard overbag made by Camp 7, which can be used alone in warm weather or emergencies. Behind it is a closely cut down bag made by Holubar, suitable by itself for most conditions. The two bags together can be used in the most severe environments and weigh less than many single bags. A rolled-foam pad, which makes a comfortable ground bed, is leaning against the rock.

another, and touring overnight on skis a few months later. A full-scale down bag that is adequate for really cold weather is too hot and too heavy most of the time, despite a price tag of a couple of hundred dollars. Besides versatility, there are several other advantages to a double system. In conditions where moisture tends to be a problem, wetness is driven out into the synthetic bag by body heat. The down inner bag stays dry, and the lightweight synthetic outer bag is very easily dried.

If a double system is chosen, it's important to note that most manufacturers don't yet understand the principle very well. If a heavy synthetic outer bag of four or five pounds is used, the system becomes far too heavy and cumbersome. The inner down bag must be close fitting; otherwise the outer bag either compresses the down or must be made very large. Probably the best combination is made up of an inner down bag that's fully baffled and very well constructed, perhaps with a weight of 2½ pounds, and an outer bag with a single layer of 7-to-10-ounce synthetic without any hood, weighing 2 to 2½ pounds. Thus, when such a combination is used, making an expedition-grade bag, the weight is between four and five pounds, considerably less than many down winter bags.

Some of the better-known manufacturers of good lightweight sleeping bags are Camp 7, Sierra Designs, Holubar, North Face, Eastern Mountain Sports, and Snow Lion. Kits are available from Frostline and Holubar.

AIR MATTRESSES AND FOAM PADS

Regardless of the kind of sleeping bag you use, it's usually necessary to have a separate ground bed, both to provide insulation and to soften the surface on which you are sleeping. Polyesterinsulated bags may require pads that are less thick than down ones, because polyester is less compressible. Almost by definition, however, any bag suitable for lightweight camping is easily scrunched down into a small space, and thus doesn't shield you very much from either cold surfaces or hard ones. If your bag is warmer than might otherwise be necessary for a particular trip, you may be comfortable without a ground bed, but the optimum combination to achieve maximum warmth with minimum weight and bulk is a sleeping bag *and* a ground bed. Besides, it's a simple fact of life that most people are used to sleeping on soft beds, not on the floor, and it takes some time to get used to sleeping comfortably on a really hard surface. There are ideal camping spots floored with soft and springy vegetation. Some of these are even lightly used so that it isn't ecologically damaging to sleep there. However, you'll spend a lot of nights on hard gravel, rock, or packed dirt, so it's better to be prepared for them. Counting on perfect campsites is like depending on always having balmy, rainless weather.

Air mattresses are extremely good for smoothing out rough ground, and they are very compact when deflated. However, most of the ones on the market are either too heavy or too flimsy for use in lightweight camping. Rubberized nylon models are available for lightweight campers who prefer air mattresses. They tend to be a little heavier than covered foam pads, but otherwise they're excellent. The thin, inexpensive vinyl mattresses develop leaks and deteriorate very quickly, even when given inordinate care. Moderately successful mattresses have been made with unconnected and replaceable vinyl tubes in a nylon covering, but they tend to become brittle in cold weather. Some people find air mattresses so comfortable that they're willing to put up with their disadvantages, but others don't like the sensation of instability, the feeling that they're riding the mattresses more than resting on them.

Aside from their inherent comfort, which is a matter of taste, the greatest advantages of air mattresses are their compactness for packing, their thickness, and their watertightness, which make them very useful in wet conditions. They can also be used for flotation on water trips. Their biggest disadvantages are their tendency to develop leaks at the most inconvenient times and the fact that they are not good insulators. In cold weather the air currents that circulate inside the mattress carry away a lot of body heat. Hard-core air-mattress advocates can search out or make a mattress insulated with down inside or use a combination of foam pad and mattress, but most campers prefer foam pads of some sort, at least in cold weather.

At the opposite pole from air mattresses are *closed-cell foam pads,* providing maximum insulation for a minimum of weight and expense. A closed-cell foam is one in which each individual gas bubble is sealed off from others, preventing absorption of water and also providing extremely efficient insulation. There are many types of closed-cell foams, some more suitable for sleeping pads than others. The traditional one for the purpose is called Ensolite and is made by Uniroyal. The type with medium hardness is most suitable for sleeping pads, and is widely available from backpacking stores. The best such closed-cell foam at the time of this writing is Volarafoam, marketed by Eastern Mountain Sports, which weighs half as much as Ensolite and doesn't stiffen at low temperatures as Ensolite does. It's also cheaper. Closed-cell foam pads ¼-inch thick are adequate for summer insulation, though they don't provide much padding. They're probably about right for those who have synthetic bags and don't need a lot of padding, as well as for spartan types. Foam ⅜-inch thick is suitable for most purposes and for sleeping on snow with some heat loss, while ½-inch thickness provides quite a bit of padding and just about all the insulation anyone ever needs.

The solution preferred by most lightweight campers for warmth and comfort is an *open-cell foam pad* made up of soft polyurethane foam 1½ inches or 2 inches thick with a cover to prevent water absorption. Coated nylon is normally used as a bottom cover (next to the ground) and may be used for the top also, though some incorporate cotton or a polyester-cotton mixture on top to reduce condensation and slipperiness. Open-cell foam is like a sponge and absorbs water, and it's also easily torn and soiled unless covered with fabric. Such pads are heavier and bulkier than closed-cell pads providing equivalent insulation, but most people find open-cell pads very comfortable.

Regardless of the type of ground bed chosen, a lot of weight and bulk can be saved with little cost in comfort by using a fairly short, narrow mat. A 20-inch width is more than adequate, and a length extending from a little below the hips to just above the head is usually sufficient. This size takes care of the main weight-bearing parts of the body. Pieces of clothing, the pack, or other miscellaneous gear can be used for a pillow and padding for the feet and legs. A few experienced light-weight campers prefer to carry full-length mats, but the great majority find shorter lengths just as comfortable. Thirty-six

inches is long enough for those of average height, and 42 inches
for most taller people.

MISCELLANEOUS SLEEPING GEAR

There are a lot of little accessories or special features for the
camper's bed that are worth knowing about. Probably the most
important, as well as the cheapest and simplest to obtain, is a
ground cloth. A ground sheet protects your pad and sleeping
bag from mud, dust, pine pitch, and ground moisture. If you're
sleeping in a floored tent or a tube tent, you don't need one,
but it's worthwhile carrying one in the car for those pleasant
nights when you'd like to just crash in the nearest open space
without bothering to put up a tent. Ground cloths can be plain
or fancy, plain being a piece of plastic sheeting of suitable size,
heavy enough not to immediately fall apart but light enough
to carry. A more durable and expensive ground cloth can be
made from coated nylon fabric.

More elaborate protection for the sleeping bag can be
achieved with a *sleeping bag cover,* basically a fabric sack that
fits over the sleeping bag and is generally made from coated
fabric on the ground side and a porous fabric on the top, so
that moisture doesn't condense between the sleeping bag and
the cover. A sleeping bag cover may fit the bag closely, perhaps
with attachments to join them, or it may simply be a large rectangular sack, with room for additional equipment inside. A
sleeping bag cover not only keeps the bag from being soiled
but extends its temperature range significantly, making it comfortable at temperatures perhaps 10° lower.

A *sleeping bag liner* made of very lightweight nylon also
helps to keep a bag clean, and the liner can be removed and
washed periodically. By reducing the amount of dirt that penetrates into the down and the frequency with which the bag
itself has to be cleaned or washed, the life of the bag is thus

extended. The liner should weigh under eight ounces and be well attached to the bag to prevent its wrapping around the sleeper's legs. Of the ready-made bag manufacturers, only Holubar offers a liner that's well designed. (Both Holubar and Frostline offer kit liners.) On the negative side, liners may bind somewhat, their cost has become substantial, and they add a little weight.

A sleeping bag can also be lined with coated material, either during manufacture or by the addition of a lightweight coated liner. Such liners, first devised by Jack Stephenson of Warmlite and now being made by several companies, prevent evaporated moisture from being carried away from the body and into the insulation. It's important to note that the waterproof layer is *inside* the bag, *not outside*. This *vapor-barrier liner* serves to keep insulation dry and clean, and it's particularly useful for those who camp in extreme conditions and who are attempting to achieve very light weight. The vapor barrier not only keeps the insulation dry and efficient but also prevents much of the normal heat loss the body experiences through insensible perspiration. That's because the humidity inside the bag rapidly rises to saturation, and evaporation from the skin then stops. Some people don't find the feeling of a bag with a vapor-barrier liner disagreeable, and anyone can get used to it if they want to. However, there are disadvantages that will probably limit the popularity of the VBL bags. When his or her body begins to overheat and perspire, the sleeper either wakes up and opens the zipper for ventilation or fills the bag with sweat. Though the insulation of the bag stays clean longer than a normal bag, the initial opening of a VBL bag each morning is often accompanied by loud complaints about the quality of the released air by other inhabitants of the tent. Finally, a person using a VBL in extreme conditions can't wear heavy clothing inside the sleeping bag, since condensation tends to form in the clothes. This isn't a disadvantage with a close-fitting bag—a down parka can't be used in it anyway. Down clothing can often be used to extend the range of a larger bag, however —unless the bag has a vapor-barrier liner.

chapter 6 | **Shelter**

Except for trips on which you anticipate good weather or use lean-tos, cabins, hostels, or motels to ward off precipitation, some sort of portable shelter is usually necessary, if only as a precaution. Such shelters don't necessarily have to be expensive tents, however. A modestly priced alternative often does as well or better.

As with other items of equipment, the first step in choosing a shelter is to analyze just what you expect of it. A good mountaineering tent, which is what many people purchase whether they need it or not, is designed to protect the occupants from rain, blowing snow, and severe winds. It is made to be pitched even where there are no trees, bushes, or large rocks to use as anchor points. If what you need is protection from rain in wooded country, such a tent may not only be unnecessary but may not even be the best available choice.

The purpose of a shelter is to protect the camper from the vagaries of the weather, so that a trip remains tolerable and even enjoyable, whatever the mood of the gods happens to be when you take your trip. You need to think about the areas where you intend to go, about the normal weather pattern prevailing in the season, about the maximum severity of the weather you're likely to meet, and about discomforts you're able or willing to suffer. Tents to be used for bicycle camping, for example, are rarely required to withstand real extremes of weather; you don't go bicycle camping at high altitude in the winter, and there's no need to put up with the extra weight, bulk, and expense that a tent suited for these conditions inevitably requires. Furthermore, most cycling trips are made where you can stop at an outpost of civilization should the weather become too freakish. What's at stake if you're over-optimistic about the weather is generally your comfort, not your life. On the other hand, a mountaineer planning to use his or her tent far from civilization in severe conditions can't afford to gamble with the adequacy of a tent; it *must* be suitable for the most severe conditions that may possibly be encountered.

Discomfort and the probability of bad weather must be weighed. It's uncomfortable to get a little damp because of a barely adequate shelter, but it's also unpleasant to carry a lot of unnecessary weight around; the lightweight camper has to balance the possibility of the one against the certainty of the other. Everything from personal preference, skill, and finances to the areas and seasons in which you travel needs to be taken into account.

For example, during summer trips in the Sierra Nevada of California, I usually don't bother to carry a tent, taking a lightweight makeshift shelter instead, since rain is uncommon there in the warmer months, except for short-lived afternoon thunderstorms. I get by in less than perfect comfort in case of an unusual week-long rainy spell in exchange for the guarantee of a lighter pack. On the other hand, for a trip in the Canadian Rockies during the same months, a week without rain would be rare indeed, and I'm probably willing to put up with the weight of a tent for the extra shelter it provides.

TENTS

A tent can provide fairly complete shelter against the elements and against insects, while affording privacy in crowded camping areas. Under most conditions, a well-chosen tent is the easiest and most adequate shelter to use. A tent is basically self-contained, requiring only a flat, clear spot for pitching. Tarps and similar shelters usually require some imagination in finding supports and more elaborate precautions to allow for spilling wind and draining rain water. The operative words, however,

Figure 17 A mountain tent is designed to withstand severe wind, so it makes a good standard of comparison for other tents. A tent made for such conditions is not necessarily the best choice for other purposes, however. The wind was gusting at 90 miles an hour when this photograph was taken. The poles at each end form an inverted V, and the tunnel entrance in the foreground allows the occupants to get in and out even in blowing snow. A pack can also be stored in it.

are "well-chosen." A tent that isn't suitable for the intended use may be worse than nothing.

Mountain tents make a good starting point for a discussion, because they're designed to perform in the most severe conditions. This doesn't mean that they're ideal tents; lighter weight, more space, greater convenience, and reduced cost are often possible in a tent that doesn't have to be as strong or as weathertight as a good mountaineering tent. However, since a good mountaineering tent must have excellent characteristics, flawless workmanship, and yet be relatively light in weight, it makes a fine basis for comparison with other tents. Good examples of mountaineering tents are those made by Holubar, Sierra Designs, North Face, Gerry, and Snow Lion. Excellent kits are available from Frostline.

Severe winds are common above timberline, so wind stability is a critical feature in a mountain tent. In general, such a tent must be stable regardless of the direction from which the wind is blowing, because gusts in the alpine zone often blow first from one direction and then another. Any tent is most comfortable when correctly oriented to the prevailing wind, but mountain tents shouldn't be made so that they are stable or weatherproof only when angled a certain way. These requirements generally preclude large, steep walls or open sides. All the sides must be sloping and well tensioned or quite small so that the tent spills the wind. Loose areas of fabric that can form pockets to catch the wind are design weaknesses in mountain tents. Similarly, mountain tents must be proof against rain being blown horizontally by the wind, as well as against that falling from above.

The standard design that's evolved since the development of nylon fabrics is a double-walled tent. The inside is made of a porous material, while the outer layer is impermeable to moisture and is separated from the inner one by an air space ventilated to the outside of the tent. The reason for this design is primarily to reduce condensation inside the tent, while retaining a completely waterproof exterior. If the canopy of the

Figure 18 A standard mountain tent, like the one shown in the preceding picture, with a waterproof flysheet pitched over it for protection against the rain. The tent itself is made of porous nylon, except for the coated floor and lower sidewalls. Tents like this one are very stable and versatile, but they require many stakes to pitch and weigh more for the room they provide than some modern designs.

tent is not absolutely waterproof, hard rain will leak through; how soon and how fast it does so simply depends on the fabric used and the intensity of the rain. With the thin fabrics used in modern mountaineering tents, the leakage doesn't take long to start with an uncoated fabric.

If, on the other hand, a single layer of fabric with a waterproof coating is used, moisture from the breath and bodies of the occupants or from cooking done inside the tent will tend to condense on the inside of the tent whenever the weather is cool. Such collected moisture rapidly runs down the slick coating to the tent floor or drips off onto the occupants. Single-layer coated tents are thus unsuitable for uses like mountaineering, in which cold weather is the norm, and it's often impossible to ventilate the tent well enough to get rid of all the moisture produced. When the weather is very cold, good ventilation requires wasting precious heat, yet when there's blowing snow, the tent has to be kept fairly well closed up.

The standard double-walled tent—actually it's double-roofed—allows much of the moisture produced inside to escape through the permeable inner wall. Often the space between the two walls is quite well ventilated, so that the moisture is carried off. If it does condense on the outer wall, it's still less likely to fall back on the occupants of the tent. Some of the condensation problem is caused by the nylon itself, which, because of its slick surface, tends to condense moisture more easily and then quickly shed the droplets or frost. Still, any material does this to some extent, and the reason nylon and other synthetics are so widely used is because of their great strength for a given weight.

The most common way to construct a double-walled tent is by making a complete inner tent with an uncoated canopy and adding a light coated *flysheet* or *fly,* a separate canopy that's pitched a few inches above the first. The separately pitched tent and fly offer significant weight-saving opportunities on occasions when a complete tent isn't needed. On winter trips and at high altitude where there's never any rain, many campers carry the tent without the fly, putting up with a little extra condensation to save weight. On warm weather trips in relatively protected terrain, the fly alone may be carried and pitched by itself to shed rain, providing a more limited but very light shelter. Some of this weight loss is offset by the need to carry a ground sheet, but the combination is still quite light.

The floor of a mountaineering tent is usually made of a heavier-weight coated nylon, which is really watertight and can stand a fair amount of abrasion. The waterproof layer should extend up the sides six inches to a foot so that pooling water, blowing rain, or drifted snow doesn't penetrate readily through the lower part of the tent walls. The walls of the tent have to be steep enough to shed water and snow readily and still spill wind so that the tent doesn't act like a spinnaker when a breeze comes up. It should be as easy to pitch as possible, consistent with real stability.

Most important of all, the construction of a mountain tent must be very sturdy and reliable. Strong thread should be used in the seams, and these should be well-sewn with an adequate number of stitches per inch. One of the signs of a poorly made tent is seams with long stitches, which are faster to sew, reducing labor costs, but which are likely to disintegrate at the most awkward time. Seams with fewer than eight stitches to the inch are likely to be weak. Stitching should be neat, with equal tension on both sides (see Figure 19), and done with synthetic thread. If the needle holes are large, showing around the thread, the seams will leak.

Complete screening of openings with mosquito netting is useful in mountaineering tents, as with most others, and the netting should be easy to fasten back out of the way when it is not in use. Netting sewn close to zippers at entrances tends to snag constantly. The netting should be of rotproof synthetic material, and the smaller the mesh, the better insects are kept out. Unfortunately, finer mesh also decreases ventilation.

Several good mountaineering tents are shown in Figures 17 to 20. They're of different sizes and designs, but they share the common characteristics of this type of tent.

OTHER TENT DESIGNS

Though many of the features that are necessary in mountain tents are also desirable in tents made for different purposes, others are not. If high winds aren't likely to be a problem, then vertical walls may be perfectly suitable, allowing for higher tents that are more comfortable. Unless the tent is expected to provide a lot of warmth, it may also be possible for manufac-

Figure 19 A lighterweight version of the traditional mountain tent. One end has V poles and an entrance, whereas the other end is much lower and is pitched with a single short pole. Note the coated sidewalls extending up about six inches. This tent is a Holubar Royalight. There's a frame pack in the foreground.

turers to leave large ventilation openings, saving weight and eliminating much of the condensation problem that makes a double canopy necessary for mountaineering tents. Thus, for canoeing, bicycle camping, kayaking, and backpacking in many areas, tents made from single layers of coated nylon with adequate ventilation are perfectly suitable, and they can be roomier and lighter than mountaineering tents, if they're properly designed. In general, if a less expensive tent is chosen for less demanding sorts of camping than that for which mountaineering tents are designed, it's more comfortable if it's based on one of the traditional steep-sided designs than if it's simply a single-walled version of an A-frame mountaineering tent. Condensation is more of a problem in a smaller tent like the A-frame, and it's virtually impossible for the occupants to avoid brushing against the walls.

Alternatively, if cost isn't a problem, sophisticated variations of the mountaineering tent can either increase the room inside or reduce weight while making pitching the tent easier. Experiments have been made with hemispherical tents, hemicylindrical ones, and tents with various other shapes, some successful and some disastrous. By using very light materials, some excellent tents shaped somewhat like quonset huts have been made; they're both roomy and extremely light.

The best examples of the quonset-shaped tents, incorporating a number of other innovations as well, are the extremely light tents made by Warmlite, one of the most original manufacturers of backpacking equipment. These tents use hoop-shaped and loaded poles, held up by staking the ends of the tent. Only the main part of the tent is double-walled, and both walls are coated and incorporated into the basic tent structure, rather than being pitched separately as tent and fly. Instead of relying primarily on a permeable inner tent to reduce condensation, these tents depend on a carefully designed venting system. Cold air enters vents near the bottom of the tent, and water vapor and warmer air leave at the top. This principle works very well in many backpacking situations, but it's not very good in prolonged wet, cool weather and only moderately successful in winter. Warmlite tents hold up extremely well in wind, however, and have been used successfully by some people for serious mountaineering. Their light weight is their most attractive feature—less than three pounds for a roomy two-person tent. Their shortcomings are a high price tag and the considerable care needed by the very lightweight materials. Those who are careful with their equipment can make very light tents like this last a long time, but the tents won't withstand hard treatment. Similar tents using somewhat more durable materials are made by Early Winters.

Many other examples of tent designs could be discussed, but careful examination of materials, weight, and ventilation will tell the purchaser most of what he or she needs to know.

Figure 20A An example of a tent design with a rounded top. The poles are canted toward the peaks, so that the main tent can be pitched with very few stakes. This one, made by Holubar, has the standard separate fly. Other very light types, like those made by Warmlite and Early Winters, also incorporate the fly. All are very roomy.

Venting shouldn't rely on an evening breeze; there may not be one. Openings both high and low in the tent allow lighter water vapor and warm air to move up and out the higher vent. Except in tents so well vented that condensation problems are negligible and the tents therefore confined to forest use, it should be possible to close off the vents to exclude wind and very humid outside air.

There seems to be a welcome trend to the reappearance of some older tent designs, using modern materials and the improvements they allow. The regular mountain tent has never been more than a sophisticated pup tent, of course, but the dominance of mountaineers in the quality-tent business has tended to exclude some old shapes that are better suited for backpacking. Sierra Designs has recently brought out a fine two-person backpacking tent called the Starflight, which is essentially an updated version of the old Explorer tent.

SIMPLIFIED SHELTERS

There are a number of shelters that are simpler than tents, and with a little practice and ingenuity you can utilize them just as well as tents on many types of trips. They're usually lighter, more compact, and a lot cheaper than tents.

Tarpaulins
The tarp has been used by a lot of backpackers since long before the present explosion of interest in lightweight travel. It's an inexpensive, versatile, and effective shelter from rain, provided a site is well chosen and the tarp is pitched carefully. A tarp can be pitched in a variety of ways, often incorporating your equipment as supports—bicycle, canoe, kayak, backpack, or ice ax. There are two schools of tarpaulin users; one prefers tarps made from coated nylon material with the clear advantage of durability, while the other is satisfied with sheets of plastic three mils thick or so. The plastic sheet is replaced every few trips, when it begins to develop pinholes. Nylon tarps are

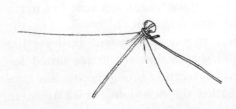

Figure 20B To provide a tie to a tarp without grommets or sewn tapes, you can put a small stone at the desired place in the fabric or plastic sheeting and tie a line around it, as shown in the drawing, so that the stone is anchored in a pocket of the tarp. The line can then be attached to a convenient tree, rock, or stake.

generally equipped with an assortment of grommets, ties, or both to help the user attach lines. Several gadgets are available to permit fixing lines to points on plastic sheeting, but you can do equally well by tying off a small stone with the parachute cord normally used to pitch the tarp.

Ponchos

The outdoorsperson's poncho has been mentioned as a piece of raingear, and the most Spartan lightweight campers make it do double duty as a shelter. The advantages of this arrangement are obvious: Not only is the poncho one of the lightest possible shelters but it also saves the camper from having to carry a couple of pounds of raingear. The disadvantages are that the space available under a poncho is rather limited and that once it's been pitched as a shelter, the poncho is no longer available for wear. In a downpour, this sort of arrangement is less than ideal, but it has great appeal for those who want an absolute minimum of gear and weight. It also makes excellent lightweight insurance both as a garment and shelter in regions and seasons where prolonged rain is very unlikely.

Tube Tents

By far the easiest simple shelter to pitch is the tube tent, which is just a tubular section of plastic sheeting or nylon fabric which can be hung on a length of parachute cord between two supports—trees, boulders, tent poles, or whatever else is available. As with tarps, the differences between the tents of plastic or nylon are mainly price and durability. Plastic tubes are cheap and don't last a very long time, though careful use can make them stand up through a fairly hard season of camping. Nylon versions should serve for a number of years, and they may have little refinements making them easier to pitch, but the price is a lot higher.

Flies

The flysheet from a tent usually makes an excellent light-weight shelter on trips when the full weather protection and privacy of a tent aren't required. Most flies can be pitched separately using stakes and tent poles or improvised supports. This versatility should be considered when you're buying a tent. Independent pitching may not be feasible with the fly of a self-supporting tent, and it's clearly impossible with a tent that has the fly attached.

The fly and poles for a tent may often be purchased separately, and this strategy can be particularly useful for those who eventually want to buy an expensive mountaineering tent, but who don't yet need it and can't afford the purchase price when buying other camping necessities. You can buy the fly and poles first for camping in mild seasons and then purchase the main tent about the time you're ready to try camping in more severe conditions.

If you plan to follow this course, you should be careful to find a tent that will be suitable later on. Look for a store or mail-order house that will sell the components separately, and choose a design and manufacturer sufficiently well established that you can be sure the tent will still be available when you want it.

Campers using shelters without floors should carry plastic or nylon ground sheets large enough to keep sleeping bags and pads from getting dirty, particularly on wet, muddy ground. When car camping with an expensive tent, it's also worthwhile to carry and lay down a ground sheet the same size as the tent floor under the tent, to help keep the tent clean and protect it from abrasion in rough roadside campgrounds. You often have little choice of sites in car campgrounds, besides frequently rolling in late at night when it's difficult to see every vagrant beverage-can pull tab that may be lying about, waiting to puncture the tent floor. The sheet also spares you the nuisance of cleaning off the floor while you're rolling the tent in the rain.

CHOOSING A TENT OR OTHER SHELTER

I mentioned at the beginning of this chapter that an analysis of your own needs is the most important factor in choosing a shelter. If you have a good idea of exactly what you'll use a tent for and if you don't have a problem with finances, spend a little time looking at what's available and then buy the best tent made for your purposes. For example, if your main use for a shelter will be on long-distance bicycle tours, then you need a shelter that's very light and compact, but that won't have to serve in extreme conditions. A tarp or a tube tent will do, or if you want a little more protection and some privacy in the roadside campgrounds where you'll often stay, you may want to buy a very lightweight but well-made tent.

Most readers are probably a little uncertain about what kind of trips they'll eventually end up taking, but find that finances are a distinct problem because of all the other purchases necessary when they begin camping. Both these circumstances are good reasons to begin with a simple, lightweight shelter, such as a tube tent, and to put off the purchase of a tent until it's needed. Tube tents provide satisfactory shelter for many camping conditions, although they won't be quite so weatherproof and comfortable as good tents. For the beginner, plastic tube tents fulfill the requirements of simplicity and low price better than nylon ones. Plastic tubes should be about nine feet long, nine to ten feet in circumference for one person, and twelve to fifteen feet in circumference for two. Plastic at least three mils thick should be used.

Those buying tents should examine not only the design but also the materials and workmanship. Small defects in tent seams can be enlarged by the wind until they become great rents. The number of stitches used per inch is important in itself and also gives a strong clue to the attitude of the manufacturer. Anything less than about eight stitches to the inch is too few. All thread should be synthetic or have a synthetic core. Points of stress should be reinforced with tape, extra fabric, or other suitable means, and the stress at each tent-line pullout should be distributed by a triangle of fabric or similar device. Poles should be strong and fit well. This is particularly important in tents that are self-supporting or have complex curves, since a replacement pole usually can't be improvised if one breaks.

Materials should be suited to the purpose intended. Heavier materials, assuming they're well chosen and the tent is well constructed, last longer under more severe wear than very light ones. On the other hand, you must carry extra weight. Very lightweight tents that are properly designed and sewn can serve well if they're handled carefully. A typical mountaineering tent uses 1.9-ounce ripstop fabric for the main canopy. (Weights of fabrics are normally quoted in weight per square yard, *before* any treatments and coatings are applied. Ripstop is a weave in which heavier yarns are woven in each direction at regular intervals to strengthen lightweight fabric.) The floor is normally of a heavier coated fabric, such as 2.7-ounce taffeta, while the fly is of coated fabric weighing 1.9 ounces per square yard or less.

Most tents currently available are treated with flame-retardant coatings to meet industry standards. This is unfortunate, since the standards were developed for canvas (cotton) tents, and the coatings' usefulness for lightweight nylon tents is questionable. (Nylon burns much more slowly.) They add expense and weight, though the additional weight will probably be reduced as manufacturers improve application techniques. Since the usual method for burning down a lightweight tent is misusing a stove, such retardancy is generally worthless; if you spill a pint of gasoline in the tent and ignite it, it burns like a torch whether or not it's been treated with retardants.

When comparing tent weights, it's best to put a tent with stuff sack and all hardware on the scales yourself, but if this is impossible, try to analyze the promotional literature carefully. Some manufacturers list the weight with stuff sack and stakes, while others omit one or the other. The type of stakes included in the weighing will affect the total a good deal, since some kinds are far heavier than others. The stakes included may be stout enough to hold the tent securely in a hurricane, or they may be the minimum required to make it stand in the front yard.

As a general rule, it's worthwhile to borrow or rent a tent of the type you're interested in before buying it. Take it out in the worst conditions you can find to see how comfortable, easy to pitch, and stable it really is. Most backpacking stores rent tents of the models they sell, partly to allow prospective purchasers to try them out. The rental fee can often be applied to the purchase price if you decide to buy the tent. You can also gain valuable experience with different types of tents this way.

chapter
7

Culinary Items

For most lightweight campers, cooking implements are among the most important pieces of equipment in the pack. The body is perfectly capable of surviving and functioning well with cold food for fuel, and there are plenty of lightweight forms of provender available today that require no preparation. A hot meal is a far more fitting way to end the day for most people, however, particularly after many hours of walking, pedaling, or paddling.

Cooking implements do not need to be excessively heavy or elaborate to provide appetizing meals. Camping food on lightweight trips is best kept simple, at least until you're used to the special tricks of camp cooking. After that, it's easy enough to add special touches if they fit your mood.

The foundation of the modern lightweight camper's kitchen is a small pressurized stove. There are several good reasons for this, but the primary one is ecological. At many campsites, there's simply no firewood available, unless you begin hacking down trees. Lightweight campers with modern warm sleeping gear tend to seek out pretty spots near timberline where wood is scarce and trees grow very slowly. Even if this isn't the case, camping is often concentrated in particularly desirable spots. With increasing numbers of people outdoors, the only way to preserve the beauty of these areas is to avoid building fires except where it can be done without damaging the ecology or the esthetic appeal of an area. The best way to insure against problems is to use a stove most of the time, building fires only when there is no question about their appropriateness.

STOVES

There are dozens of small stoves made for lightweight campers today, burning a variety of fuels. Most of them are perfectly suitable for nearly any kind of lightweight camping, and there's hardly ever any need to purchase a special stove for a particular use. The different types do have various advantages and disadvantages, however, and they will be summarized here.

Fuels

The most commonly used fuels for lightweight camping stoves are white gasoline (naphtha, Blazo, Coleman fuel, etc.), butane, and propane. White gas is more efficient in terms of the heat output for a given amount of fuel and is far less expensive to use over the long run. Butane and propane are very simple to use in most situations, since they boil at normal air temperature and pressure. This means the stove simply needs to be turned on and lit, without any need for pumping or preheating. Other fuels which are less frequently used are kerosene and alcohol.

Butane and propane stoves are very popular because of their simplicity of operation. You merely attach the correct type of canister to the stove, open the valve, and light the gas with a match or lighter. You can begin cooking immediately.

Fuss and bother are minimal. Most such stoves are very light and are initially cheaper than white-gas models. The disadvantages are that empty canisters have to be carried out and disposed of, that partially used ones can't be refilled, that canisters are expensive, that you can't obtain the high heat output available with some gasoline and kerosene stoves, that heat production drops off as a canister is emptied, and that the stoves don't function very well in cold weather. (The pressure of propane—and especially butane—is reduced when the cylinder is cold.)

Self-pressurizing white-gasoline stoves have traditionally been the standard lightweight camping stoves. White gas is fed by wick from a refillable tank to the burner and is vaporized in transit by the heat of the burning stove. Pressure is also maintained in the tank by the heat of the stove. To light the stove, it's necessary to preheat it to get the cycle started. This is usually accomplished by putting a little fuel in a cup that's part of the stove and lighting this priming fuel. After most of the priming fuel has burned the stove is turned on and vaporized fuel is ignited by the priming flame.

The advantages of these stoves are their proven reliability, the ready availability of their fuel in North America, the low cost of fuel, ease of refilling, and the convenience of carrying containers of fuel just the right size for a trip. The disadvantages are the bother of priming the stoves, rather than simply lighting them; the nuisance of handling liquid fuel; and a limit in the heat produced, which is about the same as for the better butane and propane stoves.

Pumped white-gasoline stoves are similar to the self-pressurized ones, except that they're easier to prime, are generally a good deal heavier, and have a higher maximum heat output than the other types of stoves. They're also more expensive than most of the lighter and simpler stoves. A couple of exceptions should be mentioned. The MSR stove, though it's a high-output pumped stove, is very light, because it employs an aluminum fuel bottle for a tank. The Coleman Peak 1 is lighter than most pumped stoves, though not in the class of the MSR, and it's in the price range of the small self-pressurized gasoline models.

A few other considerations may be mentioned. Any stove should be as stable as possible. Lightweight travelers inevitably find themselves cooking in awkward situations on occasion, and a tippy stove with a full pot balanced on top is a nuisance at best. Alcohol stoves are not usually a good choice for lightweight travelers. Heat output per pound of fuel is low, and expense is high. Alcohol stoves are designed primarily for use aboard boats to reduce fire hazard. (Alcohol mixes with water, rather than floating on top.) Kerosene has slightly higher heat output than gasoline and has several other advantages, but the main one is that in other parts of the world, it's far more widely available than white gas.

From a safety point of view, one can make arguments for and against nearly any of the commonly used fuels. The most important thing to note is that any of them can be extremely dangerous if they're handled carelessly. By and large, safety records are quite good for all when reasonable care is taken. Some safety precautions are mentioned in Chapter XI.

POTS AND PANS

Cooksets are widely available, and nearly any of them work satisfactorily. Aluminum nesting sets are most widely used. A set of three pots, with the largest holding about four quarts, is plenty large enough to cook for up to four people; the two smaller pans will generally serve well for one or two campers. Stainless-steel pots are more durable, distribute heat more evenly, and are easier to clean, so some cooks are willing to carry the extra weight. Still others are enamored of Teflon-coated cookware, which normally prevents food from sticking.

Lids on pots are worthwhile, and they often double as plates. The best pots have bail handles that lock in position to simplify handling, though pot grippers serve just about as well. Lightweight ladles are available and are handy for scooping out soup and stews.

Those who plan to do a lot of frying, fishermen in particular, should take a stainless-steel skillet, perhaps a Teflon-coated one. Aluminum lids will serve for an occasional frying job, but they burn food easily, don't spread the heat well, and are difficult to clean. If you carry a frying pan, take a light-weight spatula, too.

Among the most efficient setups are cooksets like the Sigg, with pots which stack on top of a stove stand and windscreen. (The windscreen encircles the stove burner, allowing air in but preventing wind gusts from blowing the flame out.) These are designed to work with self-pressurized gasoline stoves like the Svea, Primus, and Optimus, but they can often be adapted to work well with others. The windscreen is effective, and the pots are made to nest on the windscreen so that they're very stable. Check the model you're thinking of buying to make sure the fit is not too tight, though. A snug fit will become a locking one after the aluminum has been dented a little.

EATING UTENSILS

As with pots, some people carry the minimum possible in utensils, while others find the convenience of a few extra items is more important than the ounces they add to the pack. A large spoon may be carried for the kitchen, and each person normally carries at least a cup and a spoon. Many campers carry a bowl or plate for each person as well, unless the pot lids are used for the purpose, but lone campers are as likely to eat directly from the pots. Cups are most commonly made of plastic or stainless steel. Aluminum conducts heat so well that an aluminum cup filled with a hot beverage burns the lips and fingers. The steel Sierra Club cup is a favorite of many campers as an all purpose bowl, cup, and dipper to obtain a quick drink from a nearby stream. Others prefer a narrow-mouthed plastic cup that doesn't cool liquids so quickly. Plastic bowls also have the advantage of not allowing food to cool as quickly or burning your hands when filled with hot stew. They don't clean as easily as metal ones, however.

The pocket knife serves well enough for table use, and it may include a can opener. Otherwise, one of the tiny Army openers is light and effective; tie it to something or it will disappear. Some people carry forks and others don't.

MISCELLANEOUS KITCHEN ITEMS

Pot grippers and ladles, mentioned above, are particularly handy. A salt-and-pepper shaker of some sort is worthwhile. In areas where water may have to be carried some distance, a collapsible water container is worth having for camp use in addition to personal water bottles. Various plastic food containers are favored by different people, depending on availability and on the particular foods they like to carry.

Those using liquid-fuel stoves may want an eyedropper for priming and a funnel or spout top for the fuel can. A good supply of matches or a cigarette lighter should be carried with kitchen items, apart from any emergency supply.

Cleanup tools are partly a matter of taste, but they should pollute surroundings as little as possible. I use a biodegradable soap, in small quantities, and a piece of 3M abrasive pad, which doesn't rust, can be used without soap, and is light in weight.

chapter 8 | **What to Carry It In**

A pack or its equivalent is a necessity for any form of self-propelled travel, unless you're content to go as John Muir did, with only a little flour, tea, and sugar. There's a wide variety of packs available, in addition to more specialized containers for bicycle and water trips. Backpacks will be considered first, then bicycle packs and carriers, and finally dry packs for boating trips.

The number of backpacks now available is staggering, and the novice going out to buy one is likely to be overwhelmed by competing claims. To look at some catalogs, you'd think that the backpacker roamed along the trail changing packs as often as a golfer changes clubs. The variety is a real asset to the careful shopper, however, since packs are available to meet almost any conceivable need.

One pack should serve the beginner well enough on all of her or his outings for several years, excepting only bicycle tours and perhaps river trips. If the pack is chosen with a little care, there's no reason why it should either wear out or prove inadequate for a long time. Later on, it may seem worthwhile to acquire another specialized pack or two, a little more suited to particular sorts of trips, but the basic pack ought to be adaptable enough to serve almost any need.

The single most important feature of a pack is its capacity. It should be big enough to carry everything that's necessary on any trip, but no bigger. It's more difficult to distribute the load correctly in a pack that's much too large. It's worse to have one that's too small, however, because at best, you'll be forced to strap equipment all over the outside, if it can be carried at all. Though excessively large packs encourage the camper to take unnecessary items, the outdoorsperson inevitably ends up with a pack somewhat larger than the optimum for many trips if one versatile pack is to serve for everything.

TYPES OF BACKPACKS

The most basic kind of pack is simply a sack with shoulder straps attached to it, so that it can be carried on the back. Such a pack is generally known as a *frameless rucksack*. A great deal of sophisticated design goes into some of the best rucksacks, because their exact shapes can be very important in determining how comfortable they'll be. Since there's no frame between the sack and the wearer, the shape of the pack itself is critical. Despite these qualifications, however, the frameless rucksack is the simplest sort of pack.

At the opposite end of the spectrum from the simple rucksack is the *contoured aluminum pack frame*. A fairly rigid frame, generally made from tubular aluminum and contoured to match the curve of the back, is fitted with carrying straps and a sack for equipment. All manner of specialized hardware and complex suspension systems to attach the frame to the body may be included. The essential features are simple enough, however: Instead of hanging directly on the wearer's body, the

Figure 21 The beginner should be able to find one pack that will serve all his or her needs for some time, except for a few specialized ones like cycling. This frameless rucksack, made by Forrest Mountaineering, is very rugged and is large enough for a person who's willing to go light. The pack has a removable pad that goes next to the back and is made of extremely durable material, but, as with all frameless rucksacks, all the weight is carried from the shoulders. The side pockets are detachable. This sort of pack is a favorite with climbers and skiers.

bag is fastened to the frame, and that's attached to the back-packer.

In between frameless rucksacks and pack frames is a complex array of packs that incorporate more or less rigid frames in the sack itself, on the side that rides against the wearer's back. These *internal-frame rucksacks* represent a compromise between the advantages and disadvantages of the other two kinds, with positive and negative features that now need to be considered.

The contoured aluminum packframe, invented by A. I.

Kelty, provides a number of advantages which have made it the standard pack for extended trips. Because of its well-deserved popularity, it's worth considering first.

Packframes made of wood have been around for quite a while. Compared to standard rucksacks, they had the advantages of permitting good ventilation of the back, of protecting the wearer from sharp projections that would poke into the back, and of providing an easy method of carrying odd loads that wouldn't fit readily into a sack. Early frames, like both frame and frameless rucksacks, however, suspended the load almost completely from the shoulders. All three types were usually made short and deep, so a large load expanded outward from the back, levering the body backward and requiring an exaggerated forward lean to avoid falling over. Carrying a heavy burden in such a pack was hard work indeed, forcing the camper to strain constantly forward, as well as to carry the weight of his or her own body and of equipment and supplies.

The contoured frame follows the curve of the spine and extends up behind the head. It is long enough to permit the load to be carried close to the body, so that the center of gravity remains close to the wearer, avoiding the need for an exaggerated forward lean. Furthermore, much of the pack's weight can be transferred to a waistband, allowing it to be carried by the pelvis and the legs without bearing heavily on the shoulders and back. This is a real blessing for the average person who hasn't developed the muscle strength and toughness necessary to comfortably carry a heavy pack with shoulder straps alone.

The contoured frame thus has a lot of advantages as an all-around pack. It permits carrying heavy loads fairly easily, because the weight can be kept close to the back and borne mainly by the hips. Placement of the load where you wish and carrying of awkward duffel are simpler because of the facility of tying or strapping nearly anything to the frame. Finally, the construction of packbags to fit frames is quite straightforward, so a frame pack of reasonable quality can be made cheaper than a pack of similar capacity with an internal frame. These days, in fact, it's difficult to buy even a good frameless rucksack for a price lower than that of an adequate frame and bag.

Contoured frame packs have disadvantages as well. A frame tends to be bulky and constricting, even when it's used with a small load. By contrast, some internal frame rucksacks, which permit the same transfer of weight to the hips and have the same large capacity as the frame packs, can be cinched down and used comfortably for small loads without feeling cumbersome. Frames are less than ideal for climbing and skiing, because they are strapped rigidly onto the torso, and because they interfere with backward movement of the head. Though they're quite strong when they're used as intended, the aluminum tubing can be easily damaged by determined

Figure 22 Contoured frame packs, originated by A. I. Kelty have become the standard for backpackers. They permit the carrying of large loads with relative comfort, keep the center of gravity close to the back, transfer much of the weight to the hips, and allow all sorts of ungainly loads to be strapped on.

baggage handlers. Frames are also awkward to maneuver in close quarters, such as in cars, canoes, and thick brush. The sharp corners and hardware are often damaging to auto upholstery, and they can hang up on rocks and vegetation.

The advantages and disadvantages of frameless rucksacks tend to reverse those of the pack frames. A good deal of care is required to properly pack a rucksack, so that the surface riding next to the back is smooth and the pack itself has the proper profile for comfortable carrying. On the other hand, a well-designed rucksack that's packed carefully affects the balance and movement of the wearer less than any other pack. Its smooth exterior doesn't tend to catch nearly so much on obstructions, so that it's relatively easy to carry in brush or squeeze through tight passages, and it fits readily into the corner of a car trunk or seat. It usually even survives the ministrations of baggage clerks on public transportation.

A frameless rucksack is the toughest sort of pack, because it bends rather than breaking, and because it has no hard projections inside that can rub the fabric against abrasive objects outside. This is one of the features that makes frameless rucksacks a favorite of many climbers. A properly packed rucksack can even be hauled up a rock face on a line without serious damage, if it's made of tough material and has smooth lines.

Soft rucksacks hug the body; they have no intervening frame or air space. While this feature promotes condensation between the pack and the body, it's preferred by many backcountry travelers, like skiers and climbers, who want the pack to ride as close as possible to the back and to move with the torso.

Most large-capacity rucksacks are made of rather heavy, stiff fabrics, which improve shape-retention as well as the durability of the packs. Many also incorporate foam pads in the back panels. Such a pad stiffens the pack somewhat and makes loading a little less critical by partially protecting the wearer's back against projections.

Rucksacks with internal frames are a compromise between

contoured frame packs and frameless rucksacks. The most common internal frame consists of aluminum stays or tubing sewn into pockets in the back panel of the pack, though fiberglass and other materials are also used. Such an internal frame, depending on its design, may simply stiffen the pack a little and help it hold its shape, or it may form a strong enough structure to transfer much of the load to a suspension system. One of the more elaborate packs of this type may have a full, padded waist belt and a shoulder harness suitable for carrying loads as heavy as those that can be managed with a pack frame.

The better internal-frame rucksacks still have much of the flexibility and other advantages of rucksacks, together with the comfortable load-carrying characteristics of frame packs. Ventilation of the back and protection from sharp objects are likely to be a bit better than with a frameless rucksack but far worse than with a pack frame. Odd-shaped loads can be strapped on far less easily than with the contoured frame. Adjustability of the suspension systems of the best internal-frame packs to people of different heights is better than that of any other type of pack. Many lightweight travelers prefer a large internal-frame pack as an all-purpose compromise, because it can be used with fair success for almost everything from an afternoon hike to a month-long expedition.

PICKING A PACK

Choosing a basic pack should not be too difficult if you keep your own purposes in mind while you're looking around. Think first about the size pack you need and the loads you want to be able to carry. One way to do this is to gather your own equipment together or make a selection at the store and stuff it all into a pack that seems about the right size. Be sure to include food, water, and fuel or substitute packages of the same weight and bulk. It's these consumable items that make a three-week pack so much heavier than an overnight one. Once you find a pack that's about the right size to hold what you want to carry, comparing its volume or dimensions to others' gives you a basis for judging all packs you're considering.

Volumes listed in catalogs or provided by stores are approximate at best. It's difficult to arrive at a valid figure for the volume of a pack, because it's flexible and cramming permits you to get more in. Forceful stuffing may also distort the pack enough to make it uncomfortable to carry or to threaten the integrity of the seams. Judgment of how to count overflow is also very subjective. Consider rucksacks with extension sleeves around the tops of their main compartments, for example; one manufacturer may list the volume of only the main sack, while another may include the amount that can be piled into the sleeve, yielding a 50 percent difference in listed volumes for identical packs. Careful comparison is important.

It's also necessary to have a good idea of the real utility of the volume of a pack. Compartmentalized packs that allow good load distribution and that simplify sorting and locating different equipment may also force you to use space rather inefficiently, depending on how well the items being carried fit the compartments. My first frame pack had no convenient spot where my cook kit could be packed without using up a lot of extra space. The kit had to go right in the middle of the largest compartment, so that a lot of room in the corners was wasted.

If you're comparing the volumes of different packs, you should also be careful to note the type of pack. For instance, most frame packs are designed for a sleeping-bag stuff sack to be strapped directly to the frame just below where the pack is mounted. A pack like this with a capacity of 3,000 cubic inches carries a good deal more than most rucksacks with the same listed volume.

Once you've narrowed your choices, the best way to try out a pack is to load it up both with the maximum and minimum amounts of gear you plan to carry in it, and walk around for a while to see how comfortable it is. This gives you a far better idea of how well your equipment fits into it and how it rides than any amount of theorizing. It also gives you an idea of the convenience of the various bits of hardware on the pack. Workmanship and materials are important too, of course, and they must be balanced against price and the use you intend to make of the pack. Finally, remember that comfort is the most important criterion of all.

Some specific features that are worth looking at in different kinds of packs are mentioned in the next three sections. In general, those primarily interested in backpacking along trails and over moderate terrain will find the best bargains in contoured frame packs. Frame packs will also be the most common choice of those who aren't used to carrying packs and who expect to be hauling loads that feel heavy to them. Outdoorspeople expecting to carry ridiculously heavy loads or unusual burdens are also good candidates for frames. Competition, mass marketing, and better production methods have brought the price of frames down over the last few years, and the packs attached to them are easier to make than many rucksacks, so a large-capacity frame pack of reasonably good quality is now generally cheaper than the equivalent rucksacks with or without internal frames. This is only true of the simplest frame packs, however. Once a lot of fancy extra features are added on, the price rises to a figure usually larger than that of rucksacks of equal quality.

Campers who want the carrying capacity of a frame pack with more versatility will probably choose one of the sophisticated, modern internal-frame rucksacks. Such packs are often comfortable and easy to use in situations ranging from day use to backpacking trips of several weeks. They're equally suited for flying, hitchhiking, and ski touring. The larger packs of this type with sophisticated suspension systems to make carrying of large loads comfortable aren't cheap. They come with many small pieces of hardware and require a great deal of com-

Figure 23 Two views of an internal-frame rucksack made by Hine-Snowbridge illustrate some pack features. This pack has a back panel that opens completely with a zipper running around three sides, a design that is also found in some frame packs. Double sliders allow the zipper to be opened at any point. Hostelers, hitchhikers, and air travelers tend to particularly appreciate the ease of getting at things in this sort of pack, which also has a fairly large capacity. The loop at the bottom is for an ice ax. The rings are for tying on extra equipment, but this is less convenient than with top-loading packs. The second illustration shows the suspension of this pack. The padded hip belt is standard on good frame packs and internal-frame rucksacks, as are padded shoulder straps. These go over the shoulders and can be adjusted at a number of points, so that the pack can be made to fit persons of many sizes. Similar packs are made by several companies.

plex and expensive stitching. Prices are in the same range as those of the better contoured frame packs.

Frameless rucksacks are often ideal for people who don't expect to carry large loads and for purists who are either able to go light or are willing to accustom their bodies to carrying large loads mainly with the shoulders. Smaller frameless rucksacks or those with only light stays may be relatively inexpensive. Larger ones using the best materials and incorporating a lot of special features will be more costly, but they should also be very tough and durable. Frameless rucksacks often appeal to climbers and lightweight specialists and to people who plan to do mostly day hiking, hosteling, or walking between mountain huts or shelters. They're attractive, too, to warm-weather campers and canoeists who plan to carry some of their equipment on long trips in a duffel or dry bag but want a smaller pack for day hikes and portaging.

FRAME PACKS

The most important features of the frame pack are the frame itself, sturdy attachment of the bag to frame, and the suspension system. A lot of fancy pockets and zippers are of little use on a frame that breaks. Aluminum frames should be of welded alloy tubing, and visual inspection should reveal no flaws in the joints. Push and pull the frame; torque it by holding the bottom corners solidly against the floor with your feet and twisting the top corners. A frame ought to be able to withstand a reasonable amount of abuse. If it's too delicate to survive a little pushing and pulling, then no one has any excuse for trying to sell it for wilderness use.

Materials other than aluminum will undoubtedly be used to make successful frames in the future, particularly to make frames more flexible, to move somewhat with the body. Various plastics have already been tried, as has fairly light aluminum with special fittings at the joints. Some of these will undoubtedly serve very well, but beginners should be cautioned that many have not proved durable in the past, whereas properly made welded frames are very strong unless they are dropped on rocks and bent. There are some very good-quality frames on the market at reasonable prices, so it makes little sense to buy a poorly made frame that may fall apart the second time out. Shop around a bit and take a look at some of the frames with simple bags and suspension systems made by the best manufacturers with long experience in making backpacks, before buying something turned out on the side by a toy company.

The packbag should be attached to the frame with *clevis pins* passing through grommets in the fabric and holes in the frame, or some similar positive arrangement. (A clevis pin is like a thick, blunt aluminum nail, which solidly anchors the pack to the frame. It has a hole in the narrow end, through which a stiff wire or split ring is passed to secure the pin. A row of these pins fits in holes along each of the frame's vertical tubes.) Fabric pockets, built into the bag and fitting over the frame ends, tend to allow the bag to fall off, and they also permit the bag to shift around, so that the fabric is quickly worn through. The bag should be made of nylon material, and the seams should be well sewn with synthetic thread. Fabric edges should be finished in some way so that they won't unravel. Coated fabric is frequently used, both to provide some water repellency and to fix the fabric edges. Pack cloth should be fairly tough; it will be subjected to a lot of heavy use. Whatever method is used to close the pack should be reasonably convenient and should effectively shut out the weather. If a top flap is used, it should be long enough to go over a pad, tent, or stuff sack.

The suspension system has to take all the load. Inspect it critically for strength and durability. A simple system may be perfectly adequate, but a weak one won't be. Failures of shoulder straps or hip belts on the trail are often difficult to repair. If there's a back band near the bottom of the frame, a hip-belt failure merely puts all the load on the shoulders. If there's no low back band and a circumferential belt is used instead, failure of the belt causes the lower bar of the frame to ride on the spine, a state of affairs that is quite uncomfortable.

Different suspension systems have their own advocates; a lot depends on your build, the sort of terrain on which you travel, and the loads you carry. If you can get to a shop in your area, try walking around with different packs, loaded as they would be on the trail. A lot of stores have sandbags or other weights for this purpose. If you can't try the packs out, you'll have to engage in a bit of guesswork.

Most shoulder straps on frames are fairly similar, using a grommet and clevis pin system to attach the padded straps to a crossbar. The width should be adjustable. Unless the point of attachment is also adjustable, the frame usually fits only people within a certain height range. A few frames have shoulder straps like those shown in the photos of large internal frame rucksacks (see Figures 23, 25, and 26).

Waist bands are a lot more variable, with four main types in use at present. The original system used by Kelty is probably the simplest and cheapest; it's adequate for most people carrying reasonable loads. In this construction, a wide back band of nylon webbing or mesh or an entire back panel of mesh is stretched over the frame. The two halves of the belt come around the body from near the bottom ends of the frame and can be tightened so that the pack is held up by the tension between belt and back band. Under heavy loads, the belt has to be pulled very tight and can become fairly uncomfortable, particularly for slim people. The weight that's suitable depends a lot on the individual and his or her training. One characteristic of this system is that the pack is held fairly closely to the hips at the bottom, a factor that may be seen as good or bad, depending on the use it's put to and the individual's preference.

For heavier loads, most backpackers find it more comfortable to use a belt that goes all the way around the waist, with the pack hung from suspension points on either side toward the rear. A back band may or may not be used in addition to the circumferential belt. This type of belt doesn't have to be cinched as tight to prevent its riding down, so it tends to be more comfortable with loads that are heavy for the individual carrying the pack. The frame tends to be a little less rigidly connected to the hips with this arrangement. Some backpackers find this more comfortable, since the movement of the hips isn't transferred so much to the shoulders—which rotate in the opposite direction from the hips when you walk—but others are annoyed by the shifting of the pack.

A number of packs incorporate arms extending forward from the bottom of the frame to connect with a circumferential belt, so that the weight of the pack is suspended from the sides of the hips, a method invented by Jack Stephenson of Warmlite and copied by several manufacturers. Some people find these systems more comfortable, while others don't, and it's impossible to state conclusively that one or the other arrangement is better for everyone.

A new method of suspension developed by North Face uses a large, flexible nylon joint to transfer weight to a circumferential waistband. A number of people have found it very comfortable to carry because of the ease with which the upper and lower body can move independently. It remains to be seen whether everyone will find this system desirable and how well the joint will stand up in the field. Some of the past disappointments over plastic-fatigue failures in pack frames have made many experienced people wary. The system is expensive.

Many conveniences can be added to frame packs, but there will be no attempt to mention them all here. Various outside pockets are useful for storing small items and those things that may be needed during the day, besides increasing the capacity of the pack. A removable extension bar for the top of the frame can be used for lashing on odd items, particularly when heavy loads are being carried. Compartmentalization inside the pack is a mixed blessing, as the previous discussion indicated. Some packs are available with partitions that can be zipped in or out, and this is quite handy. Fittings sewn to the outside of the pack for strapping on accessories are often helpful.

The standard pack for a frame opens at the top, with a light aluminum bar holding the top of the pack open. The opening

is covered by a flap. This is the simplest and cheapest arrangement, and the most reliable, too. Many find it more convenient
if the back panel of the pack opens with a zipper, so that any
part of the load is readily accessible without unpacking everything. Such a zipper goes around three sides of the rear panel
and has two sliders so you can make an opening at any point
along the perimeter, as on the rucksack shown in Figure 23.
Constriction straps may be provided to take the load off the
zipper. This system has definite advantages in convenience.
The disadvantages are cost, the possibility of zipper failure,
and the fact that the compartment cannot be expanded by
raising the top flap. Some packs provide both a top flap and a
rear-panel zipper, in an attempt to combine the advantages.

BUYING A FRAMELESS RUCKSACK

The most important feature of a rucksack is its volume, because
this is far more fixed than that of the frame pack. Though one
can strap extra equipment on the outside of a rucksack, it's less
convenient to do so than with a frame, and the amount you can
reasonably add is more limited. It's important to be sure that
the pack will hold what's required, preferably by actually trying it out. If you plan to strap some items on the outside for
certain kinds of trips, then check to see that this is convenient,
that getting into the pack is still feasible, and that the whole
arrangement can be carried comfortably.

Many of the characteristics of your rucksack should be
determined by the purpose you have in mind. If you want a
daypack for carrying a few items, you don't need a big rucksack with a main compartment that holds 3,500 cubic inches.
The more common error is to buy a pack that's too small, however, so that on every trip you face a major battle of stuffing,
strapping, and struggling, in trying to get everything in.

Figure 24 Volume is one of the most important considerations in choosing a pack, particularly a frameless rucksack. This photograph shows a number of rucksacks that can be used practically for trips ranging from short hikes to trips of several days. Volume varies widely, with the Forrest Grade V on the left holding twice as much as the Hine-Snowbridge Cirque II on the right. The ideal is to choose a pack that will conveniently hold as much as you need but no more. Only real lightweight specialists can use the Cirque for multiday trips, but this is quite possible. All these packs have pockets that can be attached for additional capacity, except for the Jansport, which has large pockets permanently affixed. The two packs on the right are made from Cordura, a tough and attractive coated nylon, while the Forrest packs on the left are constructed of a vinyl-coated nylon that's probably the toughest pack material made.

If the pack is being purchased for its ruggedness, as with a climbing pack that you expect to drag up over rocks, squeeze into chimneys, and otherwise abuse, then the material should be as tough as possible. The bottom of the pack is particularly prone to wear, and it's often reinforced. Pockets on the outside are convenient, but they tend to hang up somewhat on brush, rocks, or baggage-compartment doors. Thus, packs with clean lines are preferable for some purposes. Accessory pockets that can be attached to fittings on the outside of the pack or removed when they aren't needed are one solution.

The straps on the pack should be adjustable and should be comfortable with a load. This requires that they be fairly wide (two inches or so) where they go over the shoulders and narrow where they pass under the armpits. They should be attached to the pack at the top quite close together, since the load has to be borne on the shoulders as near the neck as possible to avoid fatigue. Trying the pack out with a load and walking around the store for a while is the best way to be sure it's comfortable. If a pack is obtained by mail, try it around the house while it's still possible to return it.

Padding in a frameless rucksack is a good feature. Many of the better large packs include a closed-cell foam pad in a compartment next to the wearer's back. If the pad is removable, it can be used as a seat, as part of a sleeping pad, or as a knee pad when paddling a canoe.

Accessory patches for strapping on skis, ice axes, camera tripods, and other items are always worthwhile on a rucksack. Waist straps are found convenient by many people to keep the pack from shifting, but they usually don't serve to transfer weight to the hips. Many rucksack users don't even bother with a waist strap. With larger packs, it may be possible to get some weight transfer when the pack is stuffed rather tightly so that it takes on a moderately rigid shape. The effect is enhanced in some packs with bottoms shaped to wrap around the hips and with a compartment into which the sleeping bag is stuffed. When packed as intended, these frameless packs have carrying characteristics similar to the larger internal-frame rucksacks. For this reason, they are made with wide hip belts that comfortably transfer the weight. On the other hand, these wrap-around packs are less versatile for carrying different loads, and they tend to aggravate perspiration problems, because they hug so much of the back and hips.

INTERNAL-FRAME RUCKSACKS

In the last few years, a number of extremely well-designed rucksacks have been developed to provide large carrying capacities and suspension systems that insure comfort and allow adjustments for people of widely varying sizes. These packs combine many of the advantages of contour pack frames and frameless rucksacks. They're much superior to the Bergans-type packs like the U.S. Army frame rucksacks. Their most important feature is the same weight-transferring ability as the frames, so that the load can easily be shared by the shoulders and the pelvis. They also tend to have a slim profile, allowing much of the load to be packed high. The center of gravity of the entire pack stays close to the wearer, so that a strong forward lean isn't necessary.

For a number of years, internal stays were used to stiffen medium-capacity rucksacks, protect the wearer's back somewhat, and transfer a little load to the waist. For more control, however, the best solution was thought to be a triangular tubular frame to which the rucksack was attached. Gradually, however, better internal frames were developed by Gerry and others. Probably the first pack to transfer the weight to the hips as well as those currently available was North Face's Ruthsack; that model also introduced the two-way zipper that opens the whole rear panel of the pack. Further refinements have been made by others, particularly Lowe Alpine Systems.

Internal-frame rucksacks designed for carrying relatively heavy loads should have fully adjustable suspension systems. Any such system should include a wide waistband padded at the rear and well stitched to the base of the pack as well as shoulder straps going all the way over the shoulders and attached low down on the pack. This construction distributes the

Figure 25 A large internal-frame rucksack. The amount of sewing detail and small pieces of hardware make this type of pack expensive, but many experienced wilderness travelers feel it is the best type of all-around pack. The padded waistband attaches to the padded base of the pack. The single large piece of webbing that attaches the shoulder straps at the lower rear can be adjusted for length, as can the straps and the top attachments to the pack. A strap across the chest helps take pressure off the shoulders when a heavy load is being carried. The straps along the side of the large single compartment permit the volume to be reduced when a light load is being carried, and they provide attachment points for the add-on side pocket. The capacity of this pack when the constrictor straps are loosened is very large. The internal stays form an X in the back panel.

load all the way over the shoulders and allows the pack to fit people of different sizes. These goals can be achieved by connecting the shoulder straps to a single strap in the center that can be moved up and down, or by crossing them and connecting each to the opposite lower corner of the pack. In either case, the upper end of the pack is connected to the shoulder straps by two adjustable straps. It's also desirable to have an easily adjustable and removable chest strap connecting the two shoulder straps. Two examples of this sort of harness on current packs are shown in Figs. 23, 25 and 26.

Internal-frame rucksacks are made in a host of variations. My personal preference is single-compartment packs. They're more versatile as to placement of equipment, particularly when the pack is used in many different activities. Other people, however, prefer dividers that segregate individual parts of the load where they're wanted. A sleeping bag normally goes in a large compartment at the bottom of the pack.

Figure 26 A large internal-frame rucksack in use. One of the great advantages of this type of pack, particularly to small people, is the comfort and adjustability of the suspension. This one is the Serex, made by Hine-Snow-bridge. A similar pack made by Lowe Alpine Systems, with the constrictors tightened, is shown in Figure 5.

For hosteling, hitchhiking, and air travel, the packs with rear-opening zip panels are very convenient. They allow neat packing of clothes and easy access to any part of the pack, but they're also good wilderness packs. They have fairly large capacities and survive airline handling quite well.

BICYCLE PACKS AND CARRIERS

Though a lot of lightweight camping equipment can be switched from one outdoor activity to another, cycling packs are an exception. A conventional rucksack is fine for carrying books or groceries around town on a bike, but a rucksack is just not a suitable way to carry much gear on a long cycling tour. The high center of gravity that results from carrying camping equipment on the back makes the rider–cycle combination unstable, the pack interferes with efficient and enjoyable pedaling, and the additional pressure on his or her posterior generally finishes off the aspiring cycle tourist in short order.

Packs for bicycling long distances should be solidly attached to the bike itself, leaving the rider free to provide the power. A number of arrangements are possible, but the combination which has proven nearly ideal for the great majority of trips is a set of *panniers* mounted on a rack over the rear wheel and a small *front bag* attached with a frame or rack just in front of the handlebars. Most of the weight goes into the rear panniers, so the weight is down low, where it's less likely to create a dangerous wobble at high speeds. The handlebar bag provides a little extra room, but it serves mainly as a storage area for items you want to be able to get at while riding or when stopping briefly at the side of the road. A few bulky, lightweight items like the sleeping bag can be loaded on top of the rear rack, but proper paring of equipment should keep the amount of gear there to a minimum.

Cyclists who choose their equipment carefully can travel lighter than many other self-propelled campers. They don't usually encounter the extremes of weather that may be the lot of mountaineers and ski tourers. Even more important is the fact that most cycling is done within easy reach of supermarkets,

Figure 27 Packs for bicycle camping in use. A rear rack supports a pair
of panniers and a waterproof stuff sack containing a sleeping bag and pad.
A rack that mounts on the handlebar stem extension holds the front bag
out of the way of the hands. Regular camping equipment is carried in the
panniers, and things that should be easy to reach, in the front bag. The
hardware attaching bicycle packs to the bike is important, because of the
potentially disastrous consequences if something works loose and goes into
the wheel. The packs shown here are made by Hine-Snowbridge. Other
good examples are made by the Touring Cyclist Shop and sold in kit form
by Frostline.

so that the amount of food that must be carried is only rarely
more than a couple of days' supply. Even this quantity is
greater than is frequently necessary. Traveling light is particularly worthwhile for the cyclist, because extra weight slows the
bicycle camper down much more than it does the backpacker
or the paddler.

The rear rack is the foundation of the system, and it deserves a lot of attention. It's important for the prospective
tourist to remember the consequences of rack failure. The
problems that a backpacker might experience with a broken
frame are miniscule by comparison. If a rack fails, it's likely to
be as the result of a sharp jolt, and this may well occur when

the cyclist is sailing down a mountain road at high speed. If a weld breaks and a support member swings into the spokes, the resultant spill can be really horrible.

The best racks are held up by triangular supports secured at the bottom to the dropout (the pieces in the bicycle frame to which the rear axle is clamped). Racks with only bars that clamp onto the bicycle tubes aren't strong enough or rigid enough to support a load as well, so the clamps tend to slip down. Any welds in the rack should be very strong, and the whole rack, once it's secured to the bicycle, should feel quite solid. Shake it from side to side as well as pushing down. If it moves back and forth very much, the bike will go into a shimmy at high speed.

Panniers, packs that hang on both sides of the rear rack, are used to carry the bulk of the equipment for bike trips. Most of the better modern panniers follow the designs developed by Hartley Alley of the Touring Cyclist Shop: separate bags, each hooked to the frame at the top with tension springs holding the bottoms to the dropouts or lower part of the rack; stiffeners riveted into the bags to minimize the danger of their getting into the spokes and made of aluminum to keep the weight low; and zippered, weathertight bags of coated nylon.

Unless you already have a rack on your bicycle, it's best to buy the panniers and the rack at the same time, since they form one unit and some combinations don't work out well together. Obviously, it must be possible to mount the panniers easily on the rack in such a way that they'll stay put. Check the clearance of your heel once the rack and panniers are mounted. Some combinations don't leave enough space for the pedaling foot to pass the bag without hitting, unless the bag is pushed back into an unstable position. The rear corners of the panniers should not project so far beyond the rack that vibration will swing them into the spokes. The better panniers can be mounted or removed from the rack in a few seconds. It's convenient if they can be zipped or snapped together for easy carrying when removed from the bicycle.

The front bag is also best supported by some sort of frame, both to keep it away from the wheel and to keep the handlebar clear, so that the hands can be moved around to different positions. Some racks fit most bags, while others are designed specifically for particular types. The main design feature for the front bag, other than stability, is ease of access while you're riding. Its pleasant to be able to get a little food or put on your sunglassses without having to stop riding and fuss with some awkward fastener. It should also be possible to shut the bag in the rain so that it's fairly weathertight.

Figure 28 Two excellent front bags. Each has a map pocket on top, aluminum stiffeners, and an easily accessible main compartment. Besides the zipper, the Kirtland pack on the left has a Velcro closure, while the French pack on the right closes with an elastic. Closures like this, which can be operated easily while riding, are important. A bicycle helmet is shown on the right; it's a worthwhile safety precaution.

With all bicycle packs, it's convenient to have numerous pockets sewn on to hold miscellaneous items. It's also fairly costly to add such extras. For those on a budget, it's usually best to pay for good-quality bags with solid fittings that hold them positively on the rack and ignore the fine points, such as carrying handles, extra pockets, and map compartments. Good bicycle packs are made by the Touring Cyclist and Hine Snowbridge.

DRY PACKS

On many sorts of water trips, it's advisable to pack clothing and equipment in waterproof containers, so that you're guaranteed a change of warm clothes and a dry sleeping bag after a day on the water. In most situations these *dry bags* also serve as extra flotation in case of an upset, insuring that the boat floats high in the water even after it's capsized. (Everything must always be tied in securely.) There are many schemes for protecting equipment against a soaking, and the degree of care that's needed varies with the trip. In general, the greater the risk of capsizing or shipping water and the colder the weather, the more careful you should be. It might be noted, however, that no one on a river or float trip has ever been known to arrive in camp complaining that his or her duffel was too dry!

Kayakers generally use flotation bags that are shaped to fit the ends of the boat and that can be opened at the wide end or along one side by removing a clamp or unrolling a snapped-down tunnel. Such storage-flotation bags are virtually a necessity on white-water trips, where most of the kayak should be filled with flotation material as a precaution, in case the paddler gets in trouble and has to get out of the craft.

Various watertight storage bags can be purchased from companies specializing in rafting equipment. The best ones are made from vinyl- or PVC-coated synthetic cloth. Pay attention to the sealing method. There are a number of workable designs, but good construction is important. There are still a few military surplus dry packs available in surplus stores, which will keep equipment dry at a reasonable price. One of the best is the large black rubberized delousing bag. A problem with any of these duffel-type sacks, whether they're commercially made or military surplus, is that they weren't made for carrying on long portages, for hiking on rest days, or anything similar. One answer is to take a pack frame on which they can be tied or a large rucksack in which they can be carried.

Another solution I've been happy with on canoe trips is to carry a heavy-duty vinyl-coated rucksack made by Forest Mountaineering for rock climbers. It's made of very tough waterproof material and has a coated sleeve sewn on the top that's designed to keep out blowing snow. The seams can be made absolutely waterproof by coating them with Plastic Rubber, a product that can be purchased in tubes at hardware stores. The sleeve can be used to seal the top of the pack by wrapping it with a large rubber band, folding it over, and sealing it a second time with another rubber band. The result is an all-purpose rucksack which can also be used as a dry pack.

Regular rucksacks and frame packs are often used by canoeists as well. To keep the contents dry, you should pack everything inside in two independently sealed heavy garbage or leaf bags. The sleeping bag can be protected the same way inside its stuff sack. On a long trip it's best to carry a few bags to replace the originals when they develop leaks.

part
II

BASIC
OUTDOOR
SKILLS

chapter | **How to Manage**
9 | **In the Outdoors**

Wilderness camping and self-propelled travel aren't terribly difficult, except when you seek a challenge, as in severe climbing or on very demanding river trips. If you're reasonably prudent, there's no reason you should suffer much discomfort on outdoor trips, unless you deliberately choose excursions of greater-than-average difficulty. Many people who haven't spent much time outdoors are full of trepidation at the thought of a first backpacking trip or overnight canoe excursion. Others are overconfident, skiing into the high mountains in the winter without the slightest notion of the problems they may encounter.

On most kinds of outdoor trips, there's nothing more serious to fear than a little discomfort. The backcountry is a good deal safer than the average freeway, and learning to get around in it smoothly is largely a matter of experience. With reasonably careful advance preparation, you needn't even suffer any miserable nights, given the luxury of modern equipment.

Most people getting into cycling and various sorts of wilderness trekking do so to enjoy themselves. Adventure is often a part of that enjoyment, but serious risks and desperate survival ordeals aren't usually welcome, at least on your first few trips into the backcountry. The best way to be sure of enjoying yourself and to avoid nasty situations is to start off at an easy rate, developing a little experience and judgment before you bite off more than you can chew. Even if you have a yearning to really challenge yourself and your capacities, it rarely makes any sense to do so from a position of ignorance. Taking chances that are well understood may be courageous; subjecting yourself to risks that you have no feeling for is more stupid than brave.

SAFETY

The two most common causes for people getting into real trouble in the wilderness are overconfidence and ignorance, and the two factors often operate together. A little advance checking on conditions that should be expected on a particular trip, together with a willingness to back off if trouble starts to develop, usually keeps a party out of major difficulties. It's important to realize that there are hazards in the backcountry, as there are elsewhere in life, and they call for reasonable precautions. If you should stroll across a California freeway in the middle of the rush hour without bothering to look, there would be a strong probability that you wouldn't reach the other side. If you leave on a winter trip to the mountains without proper equipment or knowledge, or point your canoe down a river you know nothing about on your first paddling trip, there's at least some chance you'll get in serious trouble.

One of the unfortunate habits taught us by our society is that we should be protected from hazards and unpleasantness by laws, rules, regulations, and their enforcers. If these measures fail, we tend to feel that someone should have done something in advance to prevent whatever unfortunate consequences befall us. At a minimum, we should be insured against as many nasty contingencies as possible. This attitude has many laudable consequences, but it also tends to make us feel that someone else should look after us, rather than assuming that we are responsible for our own welfare.

In the wilderness, this protectiveness of society generally doesn't exist, and it certainly shouldn't. The backcountry is a place where you're your own keeper. There's no one standing at the trailhead to tell you that you're not adequately equipped for the conditions and may not proceed. You're responsible for your own safety, and you should be. Anyone who feels the need of a ranger to look after him should return immediately to the city. One of the main attractions of the wilderness is the lack of artificial rules designed to protect us from ourselves. (There are bureaucrats and public-spirited citizens who would like to change all this, carefully regulating our use of the wilderness for our own safety. It may be hoped that they will burn on a pyre made of their own paper.)

Safety is largely a product of attitude and preparation. If you temper your ambitions by considering the limits of your experience and remember that your life may depend on your equipment and your actions, you're unlikely to encounter unexpected dangers.

HAVING FUN

The enjoyment of a trip is a subjective experience, and as a consequence, no one else can tell you what the best approach is. A lot of people are most likely to enjoy their first encounters with the backcountry if they don't have to go through a lot of hardship in the process. Others prefer an encounter with a bit more difficulty and somewhat less comfort. Be honest with yourself, and try to pick your trips accordingly. If you don't need to prove how tough you are, then choose a modest itinerary. You'll enjoy the evening in camp a lot more if you don't arrive exhausted at the end of the day. Take your time. There's no reason to hurry on a wilderness trip, unless you've made the mistake of trying to squeeze too much into a single holiday.

Pack well in advance, and check everything over carefully. Last-minute packing, particularly when you're a beginner, is likely to result in important equipment forgotten. Later on, you can use one of the strategies suggested in the first chapter to get your pack ready in a hurry. Take everything you really need, but try to draw the line there. Lightness of pack, panniers, or kayak will greatly increase your enjoyment of the trip. This is particularly true for beginners, who aren't used to heavy loads.

When you're traveling with other people, it's important to consider their enjoyment as well as your own. If you're the strongest and most experienced member of the party, remember to temper your ambitions with some thought of the rest

Figure 29 The point of lightweight camping is to have a good time. Mount McKinley National Park in the spring. The headnets worn by some members of the party are protection against mosquitoes.

of the group. A trip that's easy or moderate for you may be exhausting for others, and their entire experience could be spoiled. At the same time, no one wants to feel that he or she is a drag on the entire group. If you want to take a hard trip, go with people who are capable of it and have the same objective you do. If you go with people who are less fit, make a commitment to managing the trip so that everyone has a good time.

If you're less experienced than other members of the party, be sure that the people you're going with understand your experience and level of fitness. Even among people who engage in a lot of outdoor activities there are vast differences in attitude and conditioning. Some backpackers feel that six or seven relatively level miles make a reasonable day, while others think anything less than 15 miles with an elevation gain of a few thousand feet should be finished before lunch. Try to go with people who are at least at a comparable level of fitness, and be sure they know you're a beginner. Once you're on the road or trail, don't exhaust yourself if you're having a hard time keeping up. Try your best and don't complain unnecessarily, but let someone know if you're getting really tired. If you're getting behind, be sure you know the route, so that you won't get lost. Not all experienced outdoor travelers remember what it was like to be a beginner. Do your best and keep your sense of humor, and you'll enjoy yourself as well as being welcomed back on another trip.

WILDERNESS ETHICS

Many specific suggestions are made throughout this book regarding preservation of the backcountry, but nearly all of them are a matter of common sense to anyone who thinks about conservation. Although some questions concerning wilderness preservation are complex, nearly all those directly connected with users of the backcountry are a simple matter of taking care. It's incumbent on everyone using the wilderness to tread lightly, producing as little impact as possible. Learn to use camping methods that leave little or no trace of your passage. Don't camp on fragile vegetation when the ground is soft and easily torn up. Remove your own trash and some that's left by others, and follow good sanitation practices. Obey rules that are designed to prevent environmental degradation, particularly those limiting access or use of sensitive wildlife areas, for example, mating grounds in season. Do your part politically to help retain existing open spaces.

The use of private land is a ticklish problem in many parts of the country. Access to public lands is often blocked by strips of private holdings, and many traditional routes are being closed by landowners, often because of abuse by some individuals. In other places, strips of private land have been purchased or leased by "clubs" organized specifically to limit access to public lands, mainly to obtain exclusive hunting privileges for members.

Very often, reasonable consideration of the landowner's rights and interests are enough to obtain permission to use his or her property. Take the time to ask before barging over fences, and you'll often find a friendly response. Take care not to do any damage or abuse the privilege you've been granted. Don't camp on someone's land unless you've received permission. Never build fires without first checking. Many property owners have had a number of close calls with fires started by city slickers, and they're paranoid about the danger. In cattle country, leave gates open or closed, as you find them.

Some access problems can only be solved by putting pressure on appropriate government agencies to obtain legal right-of-way for the public to reach its own land. This is particularly true where the right to cross has been specifically purchased to prevent general access. In many situations, however, reasonable consideration for local property owners prevents difficulties from arising in the first place.

chapter | **Campsites: Choosing**
10 | **And Using Them**

Picking a campsite is mostly a matter of availability and common sense, but there are a few subtleties worth mentioning from the point of view of both comfort and environmental preservation. In many circumstances, choosing a campsite may be more a question of advance planning than of on-the-spot choice. On bicycle trips in relatively crowded areas, for example, there may be no practical places to camp, except at campgrounds operated either by government agencies or commercial proprietors, though the situation is often not as bad as it seems. Similarly, in popular backpacking areas, like the national parks, campsites may be assigned, often on the basis of advance reservations. In situations like these, your itinerary may have to be worked out in advance, and the choice of sites may be up to a ranger rather than to you.

A few points will be made concerning campsites in general, before we go on to consider the matters of setting up camp and housekeeping and the special problems involved in particular kinds of camping. Perfect campsites may be plentiful on some trips but impossible to find on others. The lightweight traveler simply has to do as well as possible, given the circumstances.

The first feature that's necessary for reasonable comfort is a level spot large enough to pitch a tent, set up a shelter, or lay out sleeping bags. The more free of lumps and debris the sleeping site is, the better; naturally, roots and imbedded rocks which can't be eliminated make for poor sleeping. Sloping ground can annoy you during the night more than you may suppose, but if you have to tolerate it, try to arrange for your head to point uphill. Drainage is a feature that may not be considered by the beginner, but it's important to anticipate the consequences of a hard rain in the middle of the night. Properly constructed modern tents with waterproof floors extending up the sides will keep out moisture better than older tents. Such "bathtub floors" can be made completely watertight if you have the foresight to seal the seams with Plastic Rubber or a similar compound, but avoid testing your tent's seaworthiness by finding a site with good drainage if possible. Trenching around tents is an outmoded practice that often results in serious soil erosion; don't do it.

If you're lucky enough to have a choice of level and reasonably smooth places for a sleeping area, then it's worth looking at features that make setting up your shelter easier. Tube tents require high supports at either end, and though two trees are ideal, many other objects can be used. Cycle campers can use a bicycle with the cord wrapped around the seat post. Conveniently placed saplings or bushes may make pitching any tent easier if they're used for guying. A major problem at campgrounds along roads is that tent sites often consist of compacted gravel pads. While such spots are often eminently level and don't become excessively muddy even after a lot of rain, they're designed mainly to prevent heavy vehicles from sinking in. Such gravel pads are hard on tent floors, and they present a surface almost impervious to tent stakes. When car camping, you can carry some spikes and a large hammer to smash them into the ground in this situation, but for lightweight camping you'll have to do a lot of improvising. It may

Figure 30 An ideal campsite is an open, level, soft spot with a view. Often you may be fortunate enough to find just this sort of spot to set up your shelter.

be possible to find a few faults where stakes can be driven in, but the remainder of the anchoring usually has to be accomplished with large rocks.

Soft forest duff is almost the ideal ground on which to camp, but most of the time you must settle for something less. Be extremely careful to clear sharp objects that may puncture your tent floor, even if you're setting up camp late. Taking a reasonable amount of time to smooth out the ground is nearly always worthwhile. A few minutes spent tossing away all those small rocks and pine cones will be amply rewarded later on, when you don't have to work them out from under your shoulders through the tent floor.

Boggy bottomlands should be avoided if at all possible when you're choosing a site. Besides being damp, they're usually insect-breeding areas, and they're frequently sheltered from breezes as well. High, open ground tends to be breezier, which may be desirable or not, depending on circumstances. Valley and gully bottoms channel cool air sinking along hillsides at night, and depressions collect pockets of cold air. A clear night sky produces a very cold environment, to which warm objects radiate heat. Dew, frost, and cooling are all increased under such a sky.

Some precautions are in order when camping under trees. A windstorm may break off dead branches and drop them on your tent; pay some attention to this possibility. Prominent trees, particularly isolated ones, may become lightning rods in a thunderstorm, and they should be avoided during periods when the thunderheads are a possibility.

It's often worth noting the directions in which the sun rises and sets. There's often a difference of hours between the time the sun falls on one site and the time it reaches another a hundred feet away. An early start on a chilly morning is speeded and made more pleasant by early sun. On the other hand, if you want to sleep late, you may want to choose a different campsite.

Avoid camping in places where you'll cause a lot of damage to delicate plant life. Lakeshores are often vulnerable, and in popular areas they receive heavy use. It's often best to camp a hundred yards from the lake and walk over for an evening view, instead of contributing to further deterioration.

Alpine meadows are easily damaged, too, especially in the spring when the ground is moist and soft, and plants are just putting out their yearly growth. Injury normally occurs only with repeated use, but lightweight travelers should be sensitive to the problem. In the desert, it's important to remember how slowly everything grows. There are usually good places on bare ground, and camping there prevents harm to the flora. Pay attention to the gray or black clumpy growth that holds much desert soil together; it's an easily destroyed lichen, and you should avoid crushing it whenever possible.

SETTING UP CAMP

If you're a beginner, it's a good idea to go through a few trial runs with your equipment before taking it out on an overnight trip. This way you will learn to set up your tent before you have to do it in the rain, and you will find out about missing guylines while you can still buy parachute cord. When you do get out on the trail, try to get off early each morning and camp early. Late-night cooking and tent-pitching are no fun when you really don't know what you're doing. Things take longer than you expect on the first few tries, and everything is complicated by darkness.

Set up your shelter as though a major storm is expected; it may just arrive during the night. Having a tent blow down at two in the morning because the guys are poorly anchored or being soaked by running water in the middle of the night isn't much fun. Make sure that all stakes and guylines are

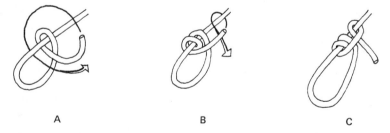

A   B   C

Figure 31   A taut-line hitch. This is a useful knot for attaching tent lines to stakes and other anchors, because it will hold in most lines when tightened, but it can be moved to adjust the tension. Tie the knot as shown, with the loop around the anchor, and then slide the knot up the line to tighten it.

firmly fixed. If it's impossible to pound in stakes at some points or if the ground is too soft to hold stakes well, use rocks or logs for anchors. Extra lengths of nylon cord are often handy to reach trees or bushes some distance away. Take the time to collect enough rocks or other weights to make everything really solid. On sand and snow, sticks or stones can be buried to provide anchors. Tent lines are easier to adjust if they are equipped with tension devices or tied with taut-line hitches.

Divide your chores if there are several people in your party. Setting up shelter, putting the gear inside or near it, cooking supper, and getting water are the most common tasks that need to be performed soon after arrival. Especially for beginners, it's well to rotate jobs, so that everyone learns how to do everything. No one should be stuck every night with the same job if he or she doesn't like it. Until you've had some practice, save your exploring and sunbathing until after the work is done. At least for your first few camps, it's very pleasant to have camp established, supper finished, and the dishes done before dark.

FIRES

Cooking and related skills are discussed in the next chapter, but since fires are built for pleasure and warmth as well as for cooking, some mention of them will be made here. Building fires is an important survival skill in which everyone who ventures often into the wilderness should be adept. Fire-building materials are among the most important items that should be carried in the backcountry to prevent trouble.

For building a fire you need a source of flame, such as a cigarette lighter or matches kept in a waterproof container; a fire starter that will burn long enough to start damp kindling; and tools for obtaining fuel. Remember that matches carried for emergency purposes—which should be separate from those carried for normal use—are only likely to be used in nasty conditions. There should be a lot of them, they should be of good quality, and a striking surface like sandpaper should be available. Kitchen matches or specially made waterproof ones should be carried. The standard *match safes* don't hold enough; carry several or use larger plastic bottles to hold matches. Butane lighters have a lot to recommend them, but they must be kept close to the body in cold weather, since they won't work when cold.

In emergency conditions it may be difficult to obtain kindling that's not soaked and impossible to find any that's not at least damp. This means that a fire starter of some sort will be necessary to make a fire; matches don't burn long enough. Various chemical pastes and tablets are available, but a plumber's candle serves well if it's protected from the wind. The tools

Figure 32 At many campsites, there's no wood for a fire, whereas, at others building a fire would be ecologically damaging. When setting up camp, take the time to anchor the tent well, and don't leave things lying about where they could get lost or wet. (The pack outside here is covered with plastic bags.) Pyramid-style tents like this one are very roomy and comfortable for families or other three- or four-person groups. The fly makes an excellent shelter for mild-weather camping. This one is made by Holubar and is shown here pitched across from Mount Mather in the Alaska Range.

required to make a fire vary with circumstances. A knife is the usual compromise, and after you've had some practice in finding dry fuel, it serves well enough in most situations. However, it should be noted that in really wet conditions, such as those occurring after several weeks of rain, about the only way to get any dry fuel is by splitting standing wood, which requires an ax. Wet conditions like this are normal in some regions.

The only way to learn to make fires reliably is by practicing. When you have the opportunity, build a fire without using newspapers or fire starters to help you. Newspaper gets damp quickly, so it would do no good in the woods even if it were available. Fire starters give the extra help you need in emergencies, but you should learn to make fires without them. The trick is to collect enough wood of all sizes, ranging from that of kitchen matches to sticks at least a couple of inches in diameter, segregated into various sizes. There are all sorts of plans for making elaborate structures to start a fire, but the main thing is to have plenty of pieces of each size. Make a stack with sticks of the smallest size, using plenty of twigs, with lots of air spaces, then light it at the bottom, and keep adding larger sticks. The mistake that nearly all novices make is to try to jump from small kindling to full size pieces too soon. When things are damp, far more care is needed, but once a blaze is going, wet wood will dry and burn.

Apart from the value of knowing how to build fires for emergencies, there's the problem of when to build campfires for normal situations. With more and more people using an ever-shrinking supply of open country, fires have become inappropriate in many areas. Nearly everyone enjoys a roaring campfire; it has a special and satisfying quality that's impossible to duplicate. A gasoline stove doesn't even qualify as a poor imitation. Nevertheless, it's important to realize that fires are a luxury in which you can't always indulge yourself on camping trips. When the wood supply is adequate, when the fire danger isn't severe, and when a fire can be built without leaving new scars, a fire can reasonably be used for cooking and as the focal point of evening activities. On the other hand, where there's no fallen dead wood, where there's a serious fire danger because of dry conditions or wind, or where a fire can't be built without charring rocks, burning the ground cover, or otherwise leaving a scar, *don't build a fire.*

There's no excuse for cutting live wood to build a fire, unless it's to save someone's life. Breaking down dead limbs and snags makes the campsite unsightly, and, in the case of trees growing in severe conditions, may harm them as much as breaking off living wood. Charcoal and carbon black will persist for tens of thousands of years. Unless you're using an already established firesite, don't scar the rocks. Build fires on bare mineral cover, preferably sand, which can be swept away after your fire is extinguished. Try to burn the wood you use completely, so that no charred chunks remain. It goes without saying that you should never leave a fire unattended. Make sure it's dead out and cold to the touch. Building a fire on duff, bog, or forest humus is very dangerous, because the fire can go under and reemerge weeks later.

HOUSEKEEPING AND SANITATION

It's a good idea to develop the habit of being neat on light-weight camping trips. Well-organized packs make camp chores much simpler, because when something is needed, it can be easily found. This is particularly true in the dark or in wet weather. Having to toss everything in the pack out in the rain to find tent stakes or food for supper is a nuisance. Everything should go into the pack or the tent at night and be protected from wind and rain. Leaving things scattered about is a good way to lose them. This is particularly important in winter camps, when a dusting of snow can cover essential equipment or an inadvertent step can press an object out of sight.

Leave your camp in such a state that the next person to pass by will see no sign of your having been there. Take your trash with you except at roadside campgrounds that have trash receptacles. Any container you can carry in full, you can carry out empty. Don't bury cans and other trash in the wilderness. You can reduce the trash which needs to be disposed of by packing food in containers that aren't bulky and hard to get rid of.

Never wash yourself or your dishes in lakes or streams. Soap and detergent pollute the water, and so does food debris, which won't normally be eaten by fish. Use a biodegradable soap in small quantities away from creeks and ponds. Small amounts of such soap soaking into the soil will be broken down by bacteria. Avoid foods that produce large quantities of waste grease.

Human waste should be disposed of well away from desirable campsites and from running water. Carry a small plastic trowel to dig a "cat hole," and include matches with your toilet paper. Dig a six-inch-deep hole in the desert and at high altitudes, where bacteria aren't active deep in the ground, and a twelve-inch-deep hole elsewhere. Burn your toilet paper before filling the hole. Obviously, when privies are provided they should be used.

SPECIAL CONSIDERATIONS

Winter campers have a whole series of special problems, many of which are discussed in Chapter XVII. One point worth making here is the advantage of finding a campsite where liquid water is available. In winter, so much time and fuel have to be expended in melting snow that it's worthwhile to make a special effort to camp near a flowing stream or a pond, in which a hole can be chopped if it's ice-covered. Around such open spaces there are often drifts that make good sites for snow caves or quarries for igloo blocks. (Wind-drifted snow is much more consolidated than the rest of the snow cover.)

Bicycle campers often have difficulty finding suitable campsites, particularly at the peripheries of large cities, where there's plenty of open country but very few sanctioned campgrounds. Farmers often allow you to camp on their land if you ask first. If you're planning to camp near a road which is adjacent to someone's land, in fact, it's a good idea to go ask even though you don't have to. The landowner is less likely to be bothered by your presence, and you're less likely to be wakened by a policeman in the middle of the night. Another way to find a camping spot is to search along superhighway rights-of-way. These are very wide, and though part of the ground is always cleared, wooded sections are often included as well. Provided you're out of sight of the road, no one is likely to bother you. The main difficulty in finding such spots is that bicycles are usually prohibited on the expressways themselves. Sites can often be spotted from roads that cross or parallel such highways, and cyclists commonly travel along the general route of a major thruway, zigzagging back and forth on secondary roads. It's amazing how much land is included in such right-of-way, and how completely unused it is.

River runners and desert campers should anticipate the possibility of rising water during the night. Gullies can be filled by flash floods generated by thunderstorms many miles away. Rivers can rise under the same influence or as a result of a water release from a dam upstream. River travelers also need to be particularly conscious of the environmental impact of their camping methods. Shorelines take a beating from campers, because everyone who comes down a river is likely to pick the same spots. Simultaneously, the ability of rivers to clean themselves out has been destroyed in many cases by dams, which prevent the high runoff and floods that formerly scoured their banks.

chapter | **The Wilderness**
11 | **Chef**

For most lightweight campers, particularly when they're just beginning to learn the pleasures of backcountry travel, food can make or break a trip. The self-propelled trekker is sure to build up a really good appetite during a hard day of pedaling, paddling, or walking with a pack, and a savory meal that evening caps everything off in a very satisfying way. On the other hand, food that's not appealing can be quite depressing after a long day's work.

This isn't to say that camping meals have to be elaborate —far from it. Simple meals are usually best, particularly for novices. Food for backcountry and cycle touring trips should be tasty, but it doesn't have to consist of culinary masterpieces. As long as there's enough food and major disasters are avoided, nearly everyone will be happy. Avoid serving the same thing every night, however, or expecting people to subsist on salami and stale peanut-butter sandwiches. Some experienced people like to go light on many trips by taking only cold food, but nothing is better calculated to turn a newcomer off. If you don't feel confident about your cooking, try out your prospective dishes in advance at home to be sure they work.

The basis of most lightweight cooking is the casserole,

stew, or soup, which can be cooked in a single pot with a fair amount of fluid, thus simplifying preparation and cleanup. Meals of this sort can be easily prepared on a small pressurized stove, when a fire isn't suitable. The likelihood of burning the food is reduced if enough water is added. The skill needed to keep track of multiple courses and juggle them so that everything is done when it's needed is eliminated. Furthermore, only a few pots have to be carried, and often only one is dirtied, with a second used only to heat water for beverages. Of course, those who wish can engage in extravaganzas, sometimes with many side dishes. Even if you enjoy elaborate camp cooking, however, one-pot meals are still likely to be welcome on those nights when you reach camp after dark in the rain and want food rather than diversion.

ORGANIZATION

The key to getting meals prepared quickly and with a minimum of confusion is to have the kitchen reasonably well organized, just as you have at home. If you need to look in half a dozen places to find a can of tomato paste, while the rest of the meal is burning, you'll have difficulty cooking at home. The same is true when you're preparing meals in camp. Things should be arranged in the pack or packs in an orderly manner and laid out so that everything is at hand before you start cooking. Obtain the water, fuel, and other things you may need beforehand. It's often most convenient for one person to get water and another to find wood if a fire is to be used for cooking, while the cook unpacks utensils and food.

All the small items related to cooking should be packed together, perhaps inside the pots. Cooking utensils, hot-pan holders, seasonings, stove accessories, and beverage makings like tea, coffee, and bouillon are best kept in a small stuff sack or

Figure 33 Much of the finest country for backpacking, like this high terrain in Yosemite National Park, is too heavily used to justify cooking fires. Take a stove, and use it unless you are sure that a fire won't be damaging.

plastic bag. The food itself may be carried by one person in a group on a short trip, but it accounts for such a large portion of the total weight on a longer outing that it must be distributed among all members.

There are many schemes for packaging the food, and the longer the trip is, the more carefully this needs to be arranged. Beginners should normally pack food in a fairly organized way, so that nothing is forgotten. Condiments which are used in many meals are usually carried separately. Salt, pepper, sugar, powdered cream substitute, and the like fall into this category. Some outdoor travelers carry herbs and spices the same way, while others add them to individual meals before the trip. Each supper is most conveniently packed together in one bag, which may then be carried as is, or combined with the rest of that day's food. One person may plan all the meals, or the chore may be shared. With the latter method, a division of labor is quite conveniently arranged: If the meals are evenly divided, each person carries the ones he or she purchased and prepares them, and the expense is already apportioned. Any number of other arrangements can be worked out, of course, depending on the inclinations of the party.

BREAKFAST

Breakfast is usually a simple meal, but it's one which requires a lot of attention, because people tend to be more set in their ways about it than any other meal. If you're planning breakfast for a group, be sure to check with everyone about the menu, lest you be faced with mutiny later on. Cold cereals that pack well, such as granola and Grape Nuts, are convenient breakfast foods. Dried fruit and powdered milk can be mixed with them in advance, and sugar, brown sugar, or honey can be carried for sweetening. Pack everything in doubled plastic bags to protect against puncturing. Honey can be purchased in unbreakable plastic squeeze containers, but it should be avoided in cold weather.

Most people take the trouble to heat water for cocoa, tea, or coffee in the morning, but it may or may not be worth dirtying pans to cook an elaborate hot breakfast. A compromise solution is to carry instant hot cereals. These require only the addition of hot water, but no cooking, so you need only make a pot of boiling water for both hot drinks and cereal, each person mixing up a portion in a bowl or cup. Instant oatmeal, wheat cereals, and hominy grits are all available. The grits are unfamiliar to most, but they're usually quite popular. Margarine, brown sugar, raisins, and nuts are good additives for the cereals.

LUNCH

Lunch is usually eaten cold at a convenient stopping place, and everything that's appetizing to an individual and keeps well is suitable. Similar foods are also usually carried for occasional snacks along the way. In fact, some people prefer a lot of small food stops to one big lunch, on the theory that they provide a constant supply of food to the body without requiring a long break for comfortable digestion. The particular plan that's followed doesn't matter much, except that those who aren't in good condition find it helpful to have a lot of snack food available. Some common lunch and snack foods are dried fruits, nuts, salami, sausages, cheese, jerky (sliced, dried meat), durable rolls, canned fish or meat, peanut butter, jams, honey, and candy.

Lunch is frequently planned and purchased individually. Since there's usually no cooking involved, it's just as easy for everyone to buy what they like and carry it themselves. Fresh fruits are always welcome for as long as they will keep, but the problems of weight and bulk limit the quantity that can be carried.

Cyclists often stop at roadside stands or stores for their lunches. Fruit, yogurt, and cottage cheese are a few of their indulgences that other lightweight travelers envy. A little dressing carried in the panniers may be welcome for a salad when you're passing through country with fresh vegetable stands.

SUPPER

There are quite a few approaches that result in satisfactory casserole-type meals for the novice. Many are sold in camping stores at exorbitant prices, but they're often quite good. Aside from price, the major problem with them is the number of portions that each allegedly contains. It can be rather difficult to convert these into realistic figures until you've gained experience with a particular brand. A reasonably accurate estimate can be made from the weight. Most of the dehydrated products packed in plastic bags consist almost entirely of carbohydrates and proteins. Items like meat bars, cheese, margarine, butter, nuts, and peanut butter have significant fat, which has more calories per unit of weight, but typical bagged meals have almost none. Carbohydrates and proteins when dehydrated have about 1,600 calories of food energy per pound. Thus if you want to get 1,000 to 1,500 calories from supper and are using such self-contained meals without adding anything extra, the supper should weigh 10 to 15 ounces per person before adding water. Naturally, if you're adding a stick of margarine or a can of tuna, dry-food quantities can be reduced appropriately.

A lot of casserole-type meals are also available in the supermarket, many of which can be made easily enough in a pot over a camp stove. Just check the directions to make a judgment. Even when the instructions say to brown the dish in the oven, this step is rarely necessary. On the other hand, adding sautéed mushrooms and hamburger requires modifications. Some steps may be combined to confine all the operations to one pot, but others are trickier. For example, you can often add other ingredients directly to water in which macaroni products have been cooked, after draining off excess water. Don't, however, start the macaroni in cold water, since the result will be a sticky gruel—edible, but less than a masterpiece.

It's simple enough to devise your own recipes for casserole-type dishes. If you're nervous about seasonings and spices, start with a dried soup, sauce, or gravy mix, and add from there. Use some sort of easily carried and cooked starch for a base: rice, noodles, macaroni, spaghetti, bulgar wheat, or dried potatoes. Dried vegetables, which can be obtained from a number of suppliers, produced at home, or sometimes bought in grocery stores, can be added along with the starch or a little before, depending on cooking times. Cheese, dried meat, canned or dried fish, nuts, or sausage can be added for protein, texture, and flavor. A little margarine adds both flavor and concentrated calories. More ideas can be found in a number of the books on backpacking and similar activities listed in the appendix.

Salads and fresh foods are welcome in relieving the monotony of dried food after a couple of days on a long trip. (Cyclists, of course, can usually indulge themselves quite often.) Avocados and tomatoes can be taken along unripe in protective containers, to ripen during the first few days. Other vegetables are more durable and keep better, and a few can be brought for a treat. Canoeists without a lot of long portages are also free to take more luxuries like these than other lightweight travelers.

BEVERAGES

A variety of hot drinks often make mealtimes at camp much more pleasant. One good solution is to provide a bag full of beverage powders, so that when hot water is ready, everyone can prepare what she or he wants. Instant coffee, tea bags or instant tea, bouillon, instant soups, and Jello are all popular.

Jello mixed with hot water makes a pleasant warm drink on chilly evenings. Don't forget to bring whatever additives members of the party may like, such as sugar and cream substitute.

Some people like to carry flavored drink mixes to add to their water bottles. They have definite advantages when chemical disinfectants have to be added to drinking water, since they help mask the taste of the chlorine or iodine. Drink mixes also lower the freezing point of the liquid, which is useful in winter. They supply calories in the form of sugar and satisfy the taste buds of those who are not used to unadulterated water. They're cheapest in the largest containers. In hot weather, particularly for those unaccustomed to it, there are some arguments for drinking the solutions made for runners and other athletes, such as ERG and Body Punch. These beverages replace the electrolytes that are lost in sweat, of which common salt is only one. Such replacement is really only necessary when you're sweating very heavily, however.

WATER

Water, in adequate quantities, is the most vital substance needed by the body, following oxygen. You can get by quite well for long periods without food, unless you become very cold, but the period during which you can function well without water is rather short. Where water is hard to find, it severely limits the range of the self-propelled traveler. A person needs at least a couple of quarts of water a day, and may need well over a gallon under dehydrating conditions. A gallon of water weighs eight pounds, so the supply that can reasonably be carried isn't large.

Suitable water containers are necessary on all camping trips, but exactly what's required varies a great deal. On a backpacking trip through mountains with many potable streams, a cup on the belt and the pots in the pack may be perfectly adequate. Cooking vessels may also suffice for the canoeist or kayaker on waters where one can safely drink directly from the river or lake. On the other hand, several gallon jugs per person may be needed on some desert trips. Careful evaluation has to be made in advance. Where water is scarce, you can hardly carry too much.

Unfortunately, most water in the United States isn't fit to drink without precautions. Pollution is more the rule than the exception, even far from urban areas. The consequences of drinking bad water are most unpleasant, so it's well to be cautious, particularly on extended trips. Water that's biologically contaminated, by animals or improper sewage treatment, can be made safe by boiling at a full rolling boil for five minutes. It can also be made safe by chemical means, preferably by using a solution of iodine in water, a method which is safer than purification with tablets or chlorine bleach. The iodine disinfectant solution is carried in a standard one-ounce bottle with a bakelite cap, available at a pharmacy. (Plastic bottles will discolor.) Buy five grams of USP grade resublimated iodine at the same time, put the crystals in the bottle, and fill it with water. Shaking the bottle saturates the water with iodine. The water from the bottle is the disinfecting solution, and it will remain at full strength no matter how many times the bottle is refilled as long as there are iodine crystals at the bottom of the bottle. (The solution is different from the commonly available liquid tincture of iodine, which leaves a quite unpleasant taste in the water.)

To use the disinfectant solution, shake the bottle vigorously for 30 seconds and add five capfuls of the solution (not the crystals) to each quart of water. Shake the water and allow it to stand 20 minutes if the water is in the neighborhood of 75° F (24° C), 30 minutes if the water is cool, or 40 minutes if it is very cold, cloudy, or known to be badly contaminated. If the solution itself is cool, add seven capfuls instead of five. (This procedure is adapted from recommendations in *Summit*

Magazine, April/May, 1977, by Fredrik Kahn, M.D. and Barbara Visscher, M.D., Dr. P.H.)

Water that's polluted with industrial wastes or with poisonous minerals occasionally found in the desert can't be purified by any means available to the camper.

STOVES AND FUEL

Some of the basic characteristics of different types of stoves were mentioned in Chapter VII, and they won't be repeated here. Most lightweight stoves sold for use by backpackers and other self-propelled campers are relatively simple and foolproof, provided you spend a little time learning to use them and that you carefully follow all safety precautions. Directions are included for lighting all of these stoves, and there's little point in repeating them here. A few points on operation, planning, and safety are worth mentioning, however.

All stoves operate at maximum efficiency for heating water or melting snow when they're turned up full. The greater the heat produced by the stove, the less fuel is wasted in the process of bringing the water to boil. So as long as all the fuel is burning, turn the stove up full for melting and boiling. Wind dissipates a great deal of the heat, even if it doesn't blow the stove out, so it's very important to shield the stove adequately from the wind. Some stoves include better shields than others, but any of them work better if operated in a sheltered spot.

If possible, avoid cooking inside your tent or snow cave. Besides the fire hazard, recent research has demonstrated that the danger of carbon-monoxide poisoning from camp stoves is quite significant.* If you have to cook inside—and it's often necessary to do so in winter or in severe weather—be extremely

* See communication from the Worcester Polytechnic Institute in *Off Belay,* February, 1976.

careful in handling fuel and in preventing the stove from over-
heating, and make sure that there's good ventilation. Try to
keep your head away from the stove as much of the time as
possible, preferably near a fresh air draft. If you use the stove
a lot in this way, consider modifying it so that the pot clears
the burner by an inch; this reduces the production of carbon
monoxide.

Liquid fuel stoves that need to be primed should be started
outside the tent, since the main danger of flare-up or spilled
fuel occurs during lighting. Don't overprime these stoves; a
little priming fuel is enough, and too much burns the wick inside and also may overheat the tank. If the stove runs out of
fuel in the midst of cooking, it must be allowed to cool before
the tank is refilled. Don't refill inside the tent. In cold weather,
be careful when handling gasoline not to spill it on your hands,
since it may be very cold. The freezing point of white gas is
below 60° F (− 51° C) and the cooling effect is increased by
rapid evaporation of the fuel from the skin.

Most popular butane stoves use "gaz" cartridges, which
can't be removed until they're empty. They should be allowed
to burn all the way down, despite low heat production during
the last 10 minutes. Don't remove the canister before it's empty,
inside a tent, or near any open flame. The standard propane,
or LP, cartridges can be removed after the stove is turned off,
but as a precaution, this should be done outside with no open
flame about, lest a valve stick open.

Any stove that overheats can be dangerous, particularly inside a tent. Gasoline stoves have pressure-release valves either
in the side of the tank or in the filling cap. If excess pressure
causes the valve to release, the stream of gasoline will amost
certainly be ignited, with spectacular results. Similar problems
can occur with cartridge stoves if the cartridge gets hot. Avoid
overpriming, and don't use pots larger than the stove is intended to handle if the bottom of the pan can reflect heat back
down on the tank. Jerry-rigged reflectors designed to heat the
tank and increase pressure are likely to push the stove past its

safety margin. The same comments apply to windshields that enclose the stove enough to create the effect of an oven. With stoves that have pressure-release valves, make it a practice to keep them pointed away from anyone's face. If you cook in a tent, think in advance how you would throw the stove out in case of trouble, and then make any needed arrangements. Cook near a door that can be opened quickly, whenever you need to cook inside a tent.

Be generous in your fuel allocations until you have learned your requirements. For one cooking group of up to four people on a trip of up to four days, a couple of canisters of fuel or a pint container of white gasoline together with a full stove should be plenty. Carry an extra canister for stoves using the little three-ounce ones. White-gasoline stoves with large tanks need no refilling on short trips. Double the fuel quantity in winter, and add appropriate amounts for longer trips or menus that require extensive simmering.

chapter

12

Routefinding
And
Weather Problems

Finding your way and dealing with bad weather are skills that you must eventually learn, to be really at home in the outdoors. Many easy trips may involve no real routefinding problems. You may spend a day walking up a trail or paddling along a lake, and simply reverse the direction the following morning. On short trips in many regions, discomfort caused by rain can be followed by a judicious retreat. It's important to improve your understanding of terrain and weather as soon as you can, however. Getting seriously lost or caught in really nasty storms can cause you a lot of discomfort, and occasionally can pose serious danger. Besides, developing well-founded confidence in your ability to read maps, navigate, and stay safe and comfortable in the worst weather is central to enjoying longer and more difficult trips.

Learning to deal with both routefinding and weather problems involves three separate considerations: development of field skills, obtaining needed information in advance of a particular trip, and taking the proper equipment along. All are essential, but the first needs the most thought, because routefinding and weather-forecasting abilities can only be acquired through extensive practice. If you develop the habits

Figure 34 This backpacker is finding his way through trailless country above timberline in cold, rainy weather. Such conditions illustrate the importance of routefinding skills and an understanding of the weather. Landmarks are plentiful in such mountainous terrain, but lowering clouds can obscure them, making map-reading skills vital. Proper clothing for the cold, wet conditions is important both for comfort and safety. Lightning would be very dangerous in this sort of place, because the hiker would be a likely discharge point.

of observation on easy trips, you'll build up the knowledge you may need to handle problems later on.

READING THE LANDSCAPE

Finding your way around always involves placing yourself and your destination in a larger frame of reference. This may be done in a variety of ways. If you're traveling by road from one town to another, you may know that your goal is 15 miles north and simply follow whatever streets you find leading north until you get there. On the other hand, you might be on a highway that you know leads to your destination and simply follow the road, without any idea of what direction you're going. In the first case your reference was directional; in the second the road formed a line of reference, though not necessarily a straight one.

All of us use various reference systems frequently every day to get around from one place to another, but we tend to take them for granted and to shift from one to another unconsciously. Similar reference systems have to be developed for any routefinding you do, whether you're bicycling on country roads, hiking through wooded country, paddling over northern lakes, or climbing a rock face.

Figure 35 Routefinding tools. The most important is a topographic map, which shows the shape of the landscape, as well as man-made and geographic features; this one is sealed against moisture in a zip-lock bag. Beside the map are a compass, which is a vital tool, and a map-measurer, which is handy for finding distances along winding trails, rivers, or shorelines.

Civilized daily life doesn't usually make us very observant about the landscape. This doesn't mean that modern women and men are oblivious to their surroundings, but rather that they tend to see patterns of roads, buildings, and signs rather than drainage systems, ridges, or stands of vegetation. A man giving me directions to his house will tell me to take the first right after passing the hamburger stand, not after crossing the creek. Developing an awareness of the changing countryside around you will teach you a great deal about finding your way, as well as being esthetically satisfying in itself. Observing and remembering your surroundings is an important aspect of route-finding, though it's also important to avoid placing false reliance on memory.

Learning to read the landscape is largely a matter of training yourself to notice the shapes of hills, their vegetation patterns, drainage systems in particular areas on both a large and small scale, shapes of the shoreline, or bends in a river. Get in the habit of looking around you, not just ahead. The only way to find out how a trail looks going the other way is to look back over your shoulder. Most routefinding skill is based on simple observation of the surrounding landscape.

MAPS

Map reading is a skill that is complementary to observation. A map is a drawn or printed summary of information that has been gathered about an area. It may be anything from a crude sketch made by the wilderness traveler along the way to the extremely detailed and accurate maps of the United States Geological Survey. Map reading is most easily learned by carrying along a good map of the area each time you go out for a bicycle ride, canoe trip, or hike, and stopping occasionally to follow your progress on the map.

Most people are fairly familiar with road maps. Anyone planning on doing much wilderness travel should become skilled at reading topographic maps, which show the shape of the terrain by the use of *contour lines*. Contour lines trace constant elevations and they're drawn at specified intervals on the map; forty feet is a common interval on a detailed map of mountainous terrain. Thus a contour line would be drawn on the map following the exact curve around each hill at an elevation of 8,000 feet, another for 8,040, one inside that for 8,080, and so on. Each fifth line is heavier, to make reading the contours easier. With a practiced eye, you can easily learn to visualize the shape of the landscape by looking at the contours on the map, and vice versa. Contour maps at various scales can be purchased at many camping stores, surveying supply houses, or directly from the United States Geological Survey, Distribution Section. For maps of areas east of the Mississippi, write to 1200 South Eads St., Arlington, VA 22202, and request index maps for the states in which you are interested; for areas west of the Mississippi write to the Federal Center, Denver, Colorado 80225. Index maps are free and give the prices for other maps. Request also the sheet which shows the symbols used on topographic maps. When buying maps, it is usually best to buy those with the green woodland overprint, which shows general vegetation patterns.

Maps of particular river and lake systems are sometimes available from the Geological Survey, in addition to the standard quadrangle maps. They are listed on the state index maps, and they can be very useful for canoeists and kayakers. Hikers generally use the normal 7½-minute maps, on which an inch equals about 2,000 feet on the ground, or 15-minute ones, on which an inch is about a mile. The latter series is more compact and covers more ground, while the former has more detail. Some regions are available in both series, while others are mapped only in one. (A 15-minute map covers 15 minutes of latitude from north to south and 15 minutes of longitude from east to west, about 17 by 13 miles in central United States.)

Roads are often not up to date on topographic maps, because they aren't revised often enough. This is especially true on the larger-scale maps that would be of the most use for cyclists, who may cover a lot of ground in a day. Some of the larger-scale topographic maps (1:250,000) may be helpful for supplementary information if you're cycling in an area with a lot of elevation changes, to enable you to find out how much climbing you'll have to do in a day. But routes should be planned with road maps. State highway departments and county road departments are normally the best sources of useful maps for cycling and for reaching hard-to-find trailheads. Cyclists usually want to travel off the main highways when possible, and information on side roads is often not included on maps designed for motorists.

THE COMPASS

The other indispensable routefinding tool is the compass. The needle of the compass aligns itself with the earth's magnetic field, and thus gives the wilderness traveler a directional reference. With it, you can orient your map, find the direction of a landmark, a trail, or a shoreline, or record the direction in which you're traveling. This independent directional reference can be vital if you lose track of your position on the map or if landmarks are scarce. Humans have no innate sense of direction, and directional references like the sun and stars tend to be difficult to use and to disappear just when they're needed.

Practice using your compass, as you do the map. Read as much as you can about map and compass work. You may find that you rarely need either one, but when you do need them, they're invaluable. To do you any good, however, they must be carried along whenever you head for the backcountry, and you must practice using them in advance.

The compass doesn't point to the north pole, nor even to the magnetic north pole: It lines up with the magnetic field around it. One piece of information shown on the topographic map is the direction a compass points in the region covered. A small figure at the bottom of the map includes a star showing true north and an arrow and degree figure showing compass north. The compass points to the east of true north in the western United States and Canada and to the west of true north in the eastern part of North America. Variations of up to 20 degrees are common.

FINDING YOUR WAY

As long as you follow conventional road and trail systems, finding your way is largely a matter of figuring out from the map and from signs which way to go at junctions. This can often be confusing enough, but the real challenge comes in guiding yourself without trails. Once you've learned to read a map and use a compass well, it's an interesting exercise to take cross-country routes, trying to end up at a particular destination. You'll learn a great deal doing this; it's good preparation for finding your way where there are no trails or where you've lost them.

Maintaining your frame of reference as precisely as possible is the key to learning to get around without trails. Keep a record of where you are on the map, the directions you travel, and the time they take. Use bearings (directions in degrees) to distant objects whenever possible. Accurate travel on a bearing can be managed easily if you can line up two distant objects. In areas of limited visibility, such as a level forest, it is necessary to find a tree or boulder some distance ahead along your bearing, picking another mark as you reach the first. It is usually a good idea to have a pencil with your map and to note all important information. Don't rely on memory until you have found exactly how far it can be trusted.

Every experienced wilderness traveler has been lost at one time or another, in the sense of being confused about his or her exact location and the proper direction to travel. However, it's unlikely that you will become seriously lost if you keep your wits about you. Being lost is relative. If you were to survive a plane crash while flying as a passenger on a long route over northern Canada, you might really be lost in the sense that you might not know your location within a thousand miles. If you have been following a trail for two hours going roughly west from a highway, however, and you lose the trail, a little thought will give you a fairly exact idea of where you are and how to find your way back. The combination of practice with the map and compass and careful analysis of the situation should get you back on track, provided you approach the situation systematically and without panic.

Each sort of terrain has its own routefinding problems, which are more amenable to solution by one technique than another. In the mountains above timberline, some plateau areas may be featureless, so that clouds and fog can suddenly rob the hiker of any points of reference. The complications of routefinding in the mountains often include difficult, dangerous, or impassable terrain. On the other hand, when visibility is good, there are always landmarks around that can be related to symbols on the map. Below the peaks, the hiker can usually find the way by following drainage systems. In fairly level woods, the problems tend to be reversed. The dangers presented by terrain and weather are greatly reduced, but there may be no visible landmarks even in good weather.

WEATHER

Weather is a constant influence on anyone living outdoors. Good weather is happiness itself, while steady rain is likely to dampen the spirits as well as equipment. In many sorts of camping, weather may be even more important, since bad weather conditions can pose serious dangers. The climber or high-country backpacker caught by a storm high on a peak may suddenly find his life seriously threatened, particularly if

he is ill equipped. Thunderstorms may present lightning hazards to climbers, canoeists on large lakes, and to hikers or
cyclists in wide, open areas.

Like routefinding, dealing with the weather requires
habitual observation, advance preparation, and a long-term
development of knowledge. Pay attention to weather maps and
patterns in the places you travel. Check long-term forecasts
before you leave on a trip, plan accordingly, and then watch
how the weather actually develops while you're there. Weather
around mountains is notoriously fickle, but it follows patterns
of its own. Learn to watch for local weather phenomena and
to understand their development and consequences. A windstorm that comes up while you are lake canoeing can present

Figure 36 Weather building up in the Alaska Range. Weather prediction
and routefinding are tricky but rewarding in tundra and mountainous
regions like this.

major problems and requires quick reactions. So do thunderheads bulging close by when you're high among peaks and ridges, because lightning strikes and produces ground currents at those high points. Cold, wet, windy weather can be dangerous for any outdoorsperson without proper protective garments, because such weather can cool the body very quickly.

Understanding the weather patterns of an area, together with some knowledge of storm systems that may be on the way, will enable the outdoor traveler to carry necessary clothing and equipment and to interpret what's happening in the surrounding air masses. If you know that a major front is on the way, deteriorating weather in the afternoon can be expected to get a lot worse before it gets better. If, on the other hand, the overall pattern is stable, you may be able to predict an afternoon squall that will clear by evening.

Routefinding and weather prediction are both crafts that the lightweight camper needs to learn as well as possible. Neither one is a really precise science with the limited tools that the outdoorsperson has at his or her disposal, and you'll never learn all there is to know about either. If you cultivate these skills, however, you'll be amply rewarded. An ability to find your way and interpret weather signs will make you feel at home in the wilderness, and the study of forecasting and navigational skills becomes more fascinating as you learn more and more.

chapter 13 | Emergencies

Emergencies on cycling and wilderness trips should be quite rare. Most of the ones that occur—and they're not common—are the result of inexperience, foolhardiness, or lack of preparation. The great majority result from a complete lack of understanding of the outdoors. Every winter in the mountains near my home in Colorado, we see a number of people who get in trouble because they go cross-country skiing, snowshoeing, or just walking at high altitudes on a sunny day with lightweight clothing and no knowledge of building shelters. The weather in the mountains can change rapidly for the worse at any time of year, and during winter in this area, winds of over a hundred miles an hour are fairly common. An inadequately equipped person who goes a long way from the road, has a mishap and breaks an ankle or a ski, or is simply caught by the weather can suddenly be thrust into a very dangerous situation.

With adequate clothing and equipment in the pack, a sudden drop in temperature and rise of the wind doesn't constitute an emergency. It may result in inconvenience or discomfort, but that's all. A real emergency is an unexpected, life-threatening situation, and it can almost always be avoided by well-prepared travelers.

This distinction between difficulties that cause discomfort or are unpleasant and those that are life-threatening is an important one to make if you run into problems on the road or trail. Many emergencies are created because people overreact to relatively minor problems. During most seasons and in most places a night out without shelter isn't an emergency. You may get cold and stiff, but the next morning you'll warm up and can walk out. Being hungry is not an emergency. For most Americans, in fact, it's probably rather beneficial, since we have plenty of stored food on our bodies that would keep us going for a long time.

Making a calm appraisal of the situation is the most important step in dealing both with unexpected difficulties and with true emergencies. Giving in to panic is a fairly natural tendency in frightening circumstances, but a fearful and unthinking reaction is usually more dangerous than whatever hazards prompted the panic in the first place. Examples of people who have gotten lost in the woods and wandered around in circles, becoming exhausted and perhaps injuring themselves, are known to everyone. In most such cases, sitting down and thinking things out would have either enabled them to find their way out or to realize that the wise course of action was to wait for morning or for help.

A cool and methodical approach, both in preparing for and in dealing with problems, is thus the key to handling emergencies. Before you leave on a trip, think about the difficulties that might arise and what you would need to deal with them. Faced with problems, take the time to think out the possible reactions and their consequences. If you're with other people, get everyone to sit down and talk the problem over, unless some people are already very distraught. In difficult situations, several minds are definitely more likely to come up with a reasonable solution. Even if other people are not think-

Figure 37 Preparation is the key to dealing with emergencies, both in terms of prevention and of solving problems that do arise. This backpacker, on a trip in the arctic tundra far from any help, has to be ready to solve any problems that may occur without outside assistance. Equipment physical condi-tioning, knowledge, and mental attitude are all important.

ing well, a cool and relaxed appraisal is almost always helpful to all.

INJURIES AND ILLNESS

Accidental injury and sudden illness are among the emergencies that may occur to anyone in the wilderness or on the road, regardless of preparation. Good sense in the backcountry is important, of course, because an injury is obviously more serious far from civilization than it would be where ambulances, hospitals, and home are within easy reach. No matter how careful you are, however, it's always possible to turn an ankle, fall and break a bone, or get sick.

Preparation for accidents may take several forms. One is simply understanding that an accident is always possible and keeping this in mind when loading the pack. Just because you plan to be back from a hike in the mountains or a bike ride before dark, don't leave your flashlight or leg light at home. Carry along enough warm clothes to keep you from becoming dangerously cold if something unexpected happens. You don't have to take enough gear to spend a night comfortably, but you should have what you need to survive.

Learning as much about first-aid techniques as possible and occasionally refreshing that knowledge is another important form of advance preparation. First-aid methods can always be considered valuable knowledge, but to an outdoorsperson, they're essential. The nearest doctor is likely to be a long way away when you're on a backpacking or a river trip. A good understanding of first aid can be lifesaving if an accident should occur to a member of your own party or to someone you meet. American Red Cross courses are available free of charge in most communities, and they provide an excellent introduction to the care of an injured or sick person. Pay particular attention to the care of traumatic injuries, treatment of shock, and improvisation of dressings and splints. When you're studying first aid, note that only a few circumstances constitute true medical emergencies that require immediate action to save a life. The major ones are severe bleeding, cessation of breathing or heartbeat, poisoning, and severe allergic reaction. The treatment of most injuries, like the handling of most emergencies, is likely to be better managed if you take enough time to think things out.

Carrying a suitable first-aid kit is the final precautionary measure that should be taken against the possibility of accidental injury and sickness. Make up your own first-aid kit, and give it some thought, rather than simply buying one ready-made. The kit should be one outcome of your first-aid training. The items you carry should be the ones you know how to use to meet specific possible emergencies that may be likely on the trips you take. The contents will vary with the length and remoteness of your travels and will depend on your own knowledge and physical problems. Many wilderness travelers who get into really remote areas take along some medicines in addition to normal first-aid supplies, to enable them to deal with the problems that may arise if help isn't available for days or weeks. Selection of such supplies needs to be carefully thought out in consultation with a physician.

When you practice first aid, it's wise to do it outdoors with a pack similar to the one you'll be carrying on a normal trip. Spend some time learning to improvise with the equipment you'll actually have available in an emergency. Pack frames can be used for backboards, and pack stays may make good splints, as do foam pads. Think about how you'd handle different emergencies, and you'll be more likely to act well if they should ever occur.

One other thing worth practicing in advance is carrying a supposedly injured person along a trail. The main reason for such practice is to gain a proper appreciation of how difficult it is to evacuate an incapacitated person. On a canoe trip, the victim can normally be paddled out, but on walking and kayak trips, a person unable to assist in his own evacuation probably requires outside help.

Before anyone goes for help, in case of an injury or other difficulties, it's vital to plan everything out carefully. Rescuers need to know the exact location of the victim, which means that it must be precisely determined on a map or that the route must be carefully marked. (A roll of surveyor's tape—lightweight, brightly colored plastic that can be tied to branches or rocks—to mark a trail is a good item to carry with the first-aid kit.) The condition of the person and what's wrong should be written down. If possible, at least one person should stay with the victim and two should go for help. With smaller groups, the best compromise possible has to be worked out. If you go out for help, remember that speed is of secondary importance; you do your friend no good if you're hurt on the way. Moreover, unless you can tell the rescuers how to reach the victim without your assistance, you must save enough energy for the return trip. Take the time to think things through. Rescues take time to mount, and the injured person will probably have to wait some time after you leave; make sure he or she has everything necessary to get along as comfortably as possible in the interim.

GETTING LOST

It was pointed out in the last chapter that being lost is a relative idea, and that in circumstances that are likely to arise in wilderness travel, a person usually knows his or her position within a fairly narrow range. (The cyclist is clearly in an even better situation.) If you sit down and consider the facts carefully, checking the map if you have one, and noting everything you know about where you are, you should be able to come up with a reasonable course of action. If possible, write down what you know, and record your subsequent actions. At least, remember everything carefully, and use some symbols scratched on something to provide a memory aid.

Clearly, if you can retrace your path, you aren't seriously lost, merely uncertain of the proper route. This may be due to earlier mistakes or false assumptions. Consider how far back you would have to go to reach a point that could be verified by taking a bearing on a landmark, finding a distinctive fork in a creek or getting some indication of your whereabouts.

If you've lost the trail, think about ways of finding it. Do you know where it runs in relation to you, so that you could easily pick up the route again by following a stream to a crossing, working up to a pass, or taking similar measures? How long has it been since you last were definitely on the trail? Work out a course that will intercept the route without fail, even if this involves time-consuming methods.

If, for example, the trail has been running roughly west and you don't know how you got off it, don't do a lot of casting about at random; you'll just get more disoriented and alarmed. Take a course back east, using a compass to make sure of directions. (A straight course can be followed in the woods without the need for repeatedly taking bearings by lining up a couple of trees, getting a third on the same line before reaching the first, and so on. In denser timber you may have to take a bearing for each leg.) Continue back for at least twice as long as you have gone since you were last surely on the trail. Make your estimate of this time carefully; use a watch if you have one, or count breaths or steps. Once you're sure you've gone back far enough, turn north or south and go for a long enough time to be sure the trail isn't that way. Then if you don't find it, turn back and go double that distance the other way. If you still don't find the trail, don't panic; just go back to your eastward course, and, after checking your analysis again, try heading north or south again. You'll tend to vastly overestimate the times you're traveling now unless you keep track of them. Moreover, you may greatly underestimate the time you traveled before realizing you were lost.

The main point of this example is that you must keep a precise record of where you go in the new frame of reference that you establish when you realize you're lost. If you run back and forth without carefully analyzing and recording what you're doing, you'll get more and more disoriented. If you keep track, you'll gain more and more knowledge as you work back and forth. You'll find where your route may be and where it isn't. Keep in mind that unless some other problem, such as severe cold or lack of water, is threatening you, you have plenty of time. Be methodical, and you'll have little trouble getting yourself out.

COLD, HEAT, AND FATIGUE

True emergencies tend to involve a whole series of events that pile up one on top of another, with the party remaining blissfully unaware that it's getting into trouble until disaster strikes. Fatigue and deterioration of the body tend to be elements of most such situations. Very often the solution is simply to stop and make camp or improvise a place to spend the night. Unless the weather or climate is likely to pose a serious threat if you stay where you are, there's rarely any good reason not to stop when people become tired, cold, or hot.

Hypothermia, the chilling of the body core, is an insidious threat to travelers in winter or in chilly, wet, windy weather. It's a special hazard to boaters and to hikers in rain and wind. A person beginning to become dangerously cold usually doesn't realize it and tends to push on to the point of collapse. He or she grows pale, perhaps blue in the lips, fingernails, and around the nose. Often the victim is testy or irrational. You should warm the person up immediately. Move into some sort of shelter as quickly as possible, remove wet clothing, and get the victim into a sleeping bag with a warm person. Warm drinks are good for a victim still coherent enough to handle them, but they provide only a little of the needed warmth. Food is important for a person starting to get chilly or recovering, but it won't be digested by a person who is seriously hypothermic. A fire is helpful both to the body and the spirit, but don't leave a victim sitting around getting worse while you spend an hour building one.

Heat can be extremely debilitating, particularly if water supplies are low. In the desert, if you're short of water, stay in the shade during the heat of the day, and travel at night if feasible. Otherwise, travel in the morning and evening. You can't last long without water, and if you become lost in the desert, water is the key to survival. Once you find some, don't go far from the source, unless you're certain of the next supply and your ability to get there. You can live for a long time in the shade next to a water supply, waiting for a search and rescue party. Without water, you may not last a day. Once severely dehydrated, you need a couple of days to fully recover, so take this into account in your estimations. Learn the indications of water close to the surface in desert areas you frequent, and carry tools to help get at it. A cottonwood grove frequently signals a source, and a small trowel and length of rubber hose aid in drawing out water.

If you begin to get into trouble, the general rule is to head for the nearest place that will provide whatever shelter you need, and then stop. Unless you have wholly miscalculated, you should have enough equipment to survive a few nights out, if you take the time to improve your shelter while you still have the stamina. For cold weather, the much-repeated advice that you should keep walking, lest you never awake after sitting or lying down, is nonsense. The cold will wake you during the night again and again, unless you've become utterly exhausted or hypothermic before stopping. The notion that you should keep going through the night when caught by cold and storm is almost always dangerously wrong. Find shelter and wait until morning or until the storm is over, unless you know how far you have to go, are sure you're not lost, and are positive you have plenty of reserves to reach your destination.

True emergencies involve unexpected combinations of difficulties, and even if this chapter were hundreds of pages long, there would be no way of anticipating all the ones that might occur. Dealing with emergencies, however, is something you can prepare yourself for by thinking about them and being ready to cope with them. People with strong mental attitudes come through emergencies toughened by the experience. A little calm reasoning will get you over most difficulties that can occur in the backcountry. Leadership that you provide your companions will get them through as well. In emergencies, people tend to regress into a dependent mental state. Consequently, the safety of a whole party can be assured by one person who keeps his or her head, or it can be threatened by one person losing control. Make sure you keep yours.

chapter 14 | Planning Your Trip

Proper planning is important for a successful lightweight camping trip, though it may range from a five-minute brainstorming session over a six-pack of beer to careful study and organization over several months. The novice has to pay particular attention to planning, because he or she is on unfamiliar ground and can't rely on past habits and experience to bring things together.

Several sorts of planning were mentioned in the first chapter in this book as efficient ways to put a trip together on the spur of the moment. Arranging packs and making lists of the equipment and supplies important to particular sorts of treks is one of the simplest forms of planning. The method is particularly applicable to weekend trips. This is true both because they're relatively short and because the areas within reach of a weekend jaunt are limited. Thus you can become familiar with the problems they present, store maps in a convenient place, and avoid extensive thinking about new problems every time you go off for two or three days.

Maps represent one of the most important aspects of trip planning. They're often the factor that determines how long in advance you must start thinking about a trip. Maps are also one of the best tools for working out the day-to-day itinerary, particularly on a long vacation trek.

Get your maps as early as you can. Stores run out of them, and so does the Geological Survey. You may have to change your mind about your destination for a weekend trip if you can't find the maps you need, and they're even more critical on longer and more remote journeys. You can go without maps, but you then may have to allow for a lot more contingencies. A map may enable you to decide on the feasibility of a three-day trip around a particular group of mountains or from one end of a chain of lakes to the other. If you want the extra adventure of doing the same trip without a detailed map, you may have to allow twice the time and carry twice the food, because you can't calculate distances and elevation gains with any precision.

Make your first few trips, whether they're backpacking walks, cycling tours, or canoe cruises by starting at one point and coming back to the same place. Next work out the distances you traveled on the map and the elevation gain up all the hills on the round trip. Combine these distances and altitude gains with your feelings about whether you worked hard or had an easy time, and you'll have a good initial estimate of how far you can plan on traveling in a day under comparable conditions. It's important to get a precise idea of these figures early in the game, particularly when you start to plan circular trips on which you return by a different route than the outbound one. You'll get plenty of opportunity to push yourself because of unexpected challenges without planning them into your trip. It's all too easy to become overoptimistic about the daily mileage that can be covered when you're "walking" on a map. Hiking on a trail is considerably harder.

When you're studying maps, get the best idea you can of the terrain, and be guided by your experience. Measure out mileages with a map measurer like the one shown in Figure 35; it has a little wheel that can be rolled along the curves of roads or trails. You can also use the side of a piece of paper carefully turned along the curves of the route. Find the true distance by the route you'll travel, not the one the birds take. Make allowances on maps that aren't very detailed for multiple switchbacks that may not be shown. Pay careful attention to elevation changes. Climbing a hill on a bicycle or on foot takes a lot longer than pedaling or walking along level ground. Significant elevation changes between lakes or sections of a river indicate falls or rapids.

Long trips require careful choice of equipment, including repair kits, and detailed planning of fuel and food. Food deficiencies on a short trip aren't of much consequence; appetites may not even catch up with increased caloric output. Over a long trip, however, insufficient food makes a considerable impression. Excess food adds a lot of weight to the pack. Reference books on food allow you to calculate caloric content; be sure you have at least 4,000 calories per person for each day on a long, hard trip. Dehydrated foods contain about 1,600 calories per pound in proteins and carbohydrates, and fats provide about double that amount.

Keep a record of your fuel use on short trips, so that you can make accurate calculations for longer ones. Make allowances if you change the kinds of food you take. Double the fuel on trips that require melting snow for water.

CROWDS

Large numbers of people are becoming a problem in many parts of the country during the popular outdoor season. It's important to find out whether a reservation or permit system is in operation at the place you plan to go. Otherwise you're likely to make a long drive only to be disappointed. Even if numbers are not officially controlled, it may be important to keep them in mind. If you pick the most popular backpacking area within five hundred miles for the Fourth of July weekend, then don't set your heart on solitude and peaceful contemplation. Get in the mood for a sociable occasion with lots of company.

If you prefer to avoid the crowds, then save your visits to popular areas for the off-seasons, which are often the most pleasant times of the year. Many places that are packed during the summer have few visitors in spring or after Labor Day and are virtually deserted in winter.

National parks tend to have heavy visitation, particularly in the vicinity of the best known attractions, the headquarters, and roads that go through the parks. Long, dead-end dirt roads are the best prospects for reaching less frequented sections. I know of parts of the most popular parks that are rarely visited. Inconvenient access and long distances are natural buffers against the multitudes. Few spots more than fifteen miles from the nearest road have a crowding problem.

Places that receive less publicity naturally are visited much less, although many of them are just as spectacular as the familiar watering holes. Take a careful look at state maps and obscure, detailed guidebooks, and you'll find a lot of fine spots where you can escape your fellow citizens. Watch the patterns followed by the herd and then deviate from them. For example, when there's a standard access road to an area, the average hiker drives to the end of the road, parks the car, and begins walking. Try taking some hikes that leave the road a few miles before the end, particularly from takeoff points without signs and parking areas. Near my home, there are dozens of examples of hiking trails where I rarely see another human being, even on days when the most popular trails are dotted with people.

Cyclists rarely find this sort of solitude, but they may want to pay a good deal of attention to routes that are heavily used by traffic, particularly truck traffic, and then avoid them. Again, reverse psychology provides the key. Look for the most direct and fastest routes between any two places where a number of people might want to go. Avoid them if possible. They're less scenic—and congested by heavy vehicles jostling each other for the right of way. Be especially wary of old U.S. highways that are still the best motor-vehicle routes between significant towns, since they're likely to be narrow and to get a lot of truck traffic. Two double-trailer trucks passing one another at sixty miles per hour on such roads leave little room for the bicycle rider.

Canoeists will find that even in popular areas like Boundary Waters, routes that require a long portage or two retain a measure of solitude. A bit of autumn frost has the same effect, and the fall colors make canoeing exceptionally beautiful.

The most important element of any trip is the company you keep. Especially on long trips, an enjoyable group can make the dullest places memorable, while incompatible partners ruin an otherwise perfect journey. The people and the trip have to mesh. A trip that would be perfect for a strong and adventurous party is almost certain to be miserable with a casual and inexperienced one.

Except on solo jaunts, which have a different sort of attraction, pay as much attention to the choice of your companions as you do to the equipment and destination. Ultimately, it's the moments shared with other people that are the most memorable experiences of lightweight camping.

part III

SELF-PROPELLED TRAVEL— AN INTRODUCTION

chapter 15 | Walking: Easy and Hard

People in the industrialized world do very little walking anymore, particularly in the United States. Walking tends to be thought of as unusual, difficult, and vaguely subversive. Perhaps it *is* subversive, given the importance of the automobile in the American economy, but it's not particularly difficult. Your body was made to walk long distances; the upright walking position is one of the characteristics of the human race. In fact, although humans compare poorly with many other animals in the speed with which they can cover short distances, we have excellent endurance over long ones, if we don't allow our muscles to atrophy. Long-distance walking comes quite naturally to us. Our ancestors did it for millions of years, and it's good for the body and the mind. A long walk relieves tension and improves the health of the heart and lungs. It's sitting, standing around, and driving automobiles that promote heart attacks.

Hiking and backpacking are particularly pleasurable sorts of walking, because they're done in natural settings, away from the domain of the automobile. Pavement is pleasant to cycle on, but it's a far less satisfying environment for walking than a trail winding through a forest, skirting a lake, or climbing a

Figure 38 Walking on all sorts of terrain is quite natural for the human body, but few modern Americans are used to walking far, particularly on rough ground. The novice hiker and backpacker has to learn how.

mountain. Walking in the backcountry can provide many joys, from listening to the descending trill of the canyon wren's song to feeling the mist as it slips up from the sea through a redwood grove. The physical pleasures of walking in the woods and fields are also more satisfying than in the domain of the internal combustion engine. Ground that yields a little at each step and that undulates is far more comfortable to walk on than cement or asphalt; during a day of walking each foot strikes the ground thousands of times, and the shock of hitting hard pavement each time is transmitted up the leg until joints and muscles ache. Dirt, turf, and humus are definitely more restful terrain for the walker.

It's ironic that a lot of adults who haven't spent much time away from the highways have to learn to walk. Going more than a few blocks under their own power can be quite tiring, particularly when the terrain and footing are irregular. Hopping from one rock to another may give them an insecure and unnatural feeling; climbing a hill is likely to be done in tiring spurts with long breaks in between, instead of a slower and steadier pace. The natural gait of the habitual walker comes with practice.

If you aren't used to hiking or walking a lot around town, plan on modest hikes for your first few wilderness trips. Those who are in good physical condition may be able to undertake a strenuous backpacking trip their first time out, but you should take it easy if you don't get much exercise. You'll probably find that you can do about half the distance when backpacking with a moderate load as you can on a day hike with a light pack.

Learn to walk at a comfortable pace. If you're in good shape, you can afford to push yourself along a little. For the average beginner, however, endurance is the greatest deficiency. Trying to move more quickly than is comfortable early in the day only brings on exhaustion that much sooner. Regardless of your physical stamina, learning to set a pace that you can keep up for long periods is very helpful. Spurting along for a short time and then stopping to rest is a tiring and not very efficient way to travel from one place to another. Stop for short rest breaks when you need them, but if they come too close together, try walking a bit more slowly and steadily.

Adjust your pace to the terrain. You can't walk up a steep grade as fast as you can cover level ground. There's no point in pushing yourself to the limit for a hundred yards and then hunching over to pant for a minute. Adjust your speed to a rate you can maintain, even if it means stopping for an extra breath at every step. You're more likely to need to do this if you are carrying a heavy pack or are at high altitude.

DAY HIKES

If you're a complete beginner, short hikes are a good way to build up your endurance and to acquire a lot of small bits of information that make long walks easier and more enjoyable. Day hikes can be easy or very hard, depending on the terrain and the distance covered. Only a few pieces of equipment are required, so hiking is a good introduction to the outdoors for those who haven't managed to acquire all the equipment needed for longer trips. There are many modest but delightful hiking areas much closer to many metropolitan centers than suitable backpacking trails, and they may be less crowded.

There are a lot of times when you can't get away for a whole weekend or spend the time needed to get to your favorite backpacking haunts. A hike in a local nature preserve, along the beach, or down a country road can be just as pleasant in a different sort of way. Try devoting some hikes specifically to learning skills like map reading and use of the compass.

Besides being pleasant in themselves, day hikes are a good way to break in your equipment without breaking yourself. You can spend time making little adjustments in your pack, finding out that your new slacks chafe uncomfortably after the first few miles, and especially breaking in your boots. If you're trying out equipment, load enough in your pack to find out what it feels like to carry some weight in it, but not so much as to spoil your walk. Everything you learn will help when you take your first multi-day backpacking trip.

CARRYING A PACK

Though the human body is quite well adapted to walking, carrying loads at the same time is more difficult. Even people who are badly out of training can generally manage to walk some distance without undue stress, but they may be hard put to carry much weight along. The muscles of the upper body can be strengthened enough to carry very heavy loads, transmitting the weight through the neck, back, pelvis, and legs. People in many parts of the world are accustomed to supporting large loads on their heads. Strengthening these muscles isn't easy for those not used to such exercise, however. Few Americans can manage to carry much weight with neck and back muscles, which is the main reason that modern packs are such a blessing. With much of the load borne directly on the pelvis through the waist strap, you can walk comfortably with moderate loads.

Proper adjustment is important. The shoulder straps should be placed as close together as possible without cutting into the neck. The waistband and straps ought to be adjusted so that a slight change in body position or the tension of the shoulder straps shifts the weight from one to the other, to relieve a set of tired muscles. The waist strap should ride on the upper part of the pelvis, so that the wide portion of the hips holds it up, and the belt squeezes against the forward projections of the pelvic bones, rather than against the waist.

Insofar as possible, it's best to load the pack so that the contents don't shift around, and so that heavy items are as high and as close to the back as possible. The higher the center of gravity and the closer to the back, the more natural the walking position can be. Heavy objects that are packed low and far away from the back force the hiker to fight against the backward pull of the pack.

Make sure that nothing is gouging against the back or rubbing uncomfortably. Small abrasions will wax large as the miles pass, so it's better not to ignore them. Otherwise, putting the pack on again after lunch or when leaving camp the next morning is likely to be a painful experience.

FEET

The walker has to pay attention to the feet. They toughen up nicely if you get out a lot, but the toughening is a gradual process that can't be rushed. The beginner has to be particularly wary, because the combination of new boots and tender feet can produce trouble in a hurry. Some people are luckier than others, because they're fortunate in the fit of their boots and have feet that are not too sensitive. No one is immune to problems, however. Some experienced backpackers are used to trouble-free walking and get very nasty blisters because they tend to ignore the warning signs.

Catching problems early is the most important thing you can do for your feet. There are quite a number of other helpful precautions and cures, but they're worthless unless they're applied before foot ailments become too serious. A spot on your foot that starts to feel sore, tender, or hot should be attended to immediately. If you make the mistake of waiting until the next rest stop, there's a good chance that a blister will have formed, been broken, and rubbed raw by then. A tender spot is easy to care for successfully. Blisters are much more difficult, and open sores are worst of all.

One of the most valuable items that should be carried by hikers and backpackers for foot care is moleskin. It can be bought in sheets at any drugstore, and consists of a thick, soft felt with adhesive backing. A piece of moleskin can be used to cover a sensitive spot on the foot before a blister occurs. If an isolated pressure point is involved, use two layers of moleskin, and cut the center out of one, so that the pressure is distributed to the surrounding area. If a blister has already started to form, don't cover the blister itself. Cut a hole the size of the blister in the center of a piece of moleskin so that the undamaged skin absorbs the pressure. Two layers may be used to thicken the protective cushion. A blister that's already broken should be treated with a first-aid cream or something similar to reduce friction, covered with a dressing, and surrounded by a pad of moleskin with a hole in the center. The whole area can then be covered with adhesive tape to hold the dressing in place.

Many other preventive measures can help avoid problems. Keep your toenails trimmed, since downhill walking can put a lot of pressure on nails that are too long. Take care of ingrown toenails, bunions, corns, and the like before you go on a long backpacking trip. Foot powder and clean socks can help prevent irritated feet. Wear your boots around as much as possible to break them in before taking them on a long trip. This practice also helps to toughen your feet.

LONGER AND HARDER WALKS

Distance and difficulty aren't synonymous. A long trip can be quite easy if enough time is taken, while a two-day trek can be tough going if it involves long distances and a lot of altitude gain over rough terrain. If you wish to keep things pleasant, work up to the harder trips gradually.

Extensive backpacking trips with reasonable daily mileage can be fairly easy, provided all participants have gone out

Figure 39 One of the attractions of backpacking is that you can travel into really remote areas, far from the nearest road and from major influence by civilization.

enough to understand their abilities and to check out equipment thoroughly. Inadequacies and weaknesses that show up several days' walk from the trailhead can result in major discomfort and difficulty. Depending on the strength of members, trips of up to a week or two away from civilization can be made with moderate loads. The weight of food that has to be carried begins to add up to a significant burden for longer trips. It's difficult to reduce the weight of the food much below two or two and a half pounds per person per day. Food for a ten-day trip thus weighs 20 or 30 pounds per person, and this must be added to equipment weight, making a load of perhaps 50 pounds. You can learn to carry a lot more, but this is about the comfortable limit for most people.

It's impossible to overemphasize the importance of terrain and other environmental considerations to the back-packer. On good trails, 12 miles a day may be a reasonable distance for average overnight hikers. Under difficult conditions, a couple of miles a day may be good progress, and only the hardy are likely to make headway at all. In desert regions where water must be carried, the weight of the pack becomes unmanageable very quickly. On arctic tundra, backpacking may be easy and pleasant in the fall, when the ground has dried and the mosquitoes have disappeared, while travel early in the year may be a nightmarish struggle through deep mud and clouds of bugs.

Whatever sort of backpacking appeals to you, it can be an inexhaustible source of recreation for the rest of your life. There are always new wonders to be seen along the most modest trails for anyone with open eyes and an open mind, and there are enough challenges for the hardiest to seek out. You need only find a trail, put on your pack, and start walking.

chapter
16

Cycling

Cycling is certainly one of the most pleasant forms of self-propelled travel for almost anyone attracted to the outdoors. It appeals equally to the hard-core fanatic, riding a hundred miles a day with camping gear, and the easygoing person who considers 20 miles a day perfectly adequate.

Unlike most of the other sports discussed in this book, cycling isn't a wilderness activity. By its very nature, it's nearly always confined to the road network of the continent, and even dirt roads are usually avoided. Cyclists were, in fact, primarily responsible for the paving of American highways, during an earlier period of the bicycle's popularity.

Bicycle touring opens up a different aspect of the country to the lightweight camper—hundreds of thousands of miles of roads that wind through woods and around lakes, over mountain passes and past the red sandstone monoliths of the desert, along the coastlines and through the valleys of the United States, Canada, and many other countries. The bicycle is the ideal sightseeing vehicle. It goes fast enough to enable the rider to cover a lot of territory, but it's slow and open enough so the cyclist can see, hear, and smell the surroundings.

There are a number of styles of cycle-touring. Many cyclists stay at motels or hotels along the way, carrying personal necessities but not cooking or camping equipment. Some groups are even accompanied by a car known as a sag-wagon driven either by a noncyclist or by the riders in rotation. Luggage is carried in the car, which is also available for broken-down bicycles or riders. Still another type of trip is one using the international system of youth hostels for shelter; but, except for the actual accommodations, this is essentially similar to staying in hotels. In fact, many people alternate between hostels and motels or hotels, either for a change of pace and expense, or because there are no hostels at some points along their route. (Youth hostels accommodate card-carrying members of all ages, generally in dormitory-style sleeping quarters.)

The emphasis in this book is on camping, and the cycle tourist who carries camping gear gains some special advantages in exchange for hauling a little extra weight. A major one is the reduced expense. After the initial investments for equipment have been made, the camping cyclist can travel about very cheaply. The only usual costs other than for food, which should be no more expensive than at home, are some campground fees and occasional small repair items, like replacement tires and cables. Provided the bicycle is in good condition at the beginning of a trip, major repairs are rarely necessary, except in case of an accident.

Perhaps the greatest advantage for the camping cyclist, however, is attaining true freedom of the roads. Such a rider isn't tied to the availability of accommodations conveniently spaced along the route, as the bicyclist staying at motels is. The bicycle tourer with camping gear can always stop at a motel or a hostel when the occasion demands—in the city, for example —without giving up the option of sleeping out under the stars for the rest of the trip. The more conventional cyclist is always dependent on the location of the next room for hire. Many of the best tours avoid areas with many hotels and motels, and in such sparsely populated regions you can usually camp almost anywhere along the side of the road.

PARING WEIGHT

It's important for those who haven't done much long-distance cycling to realize how important weight is. The bicycle rider travels relatively much farther in a day than any other self-propelled camper. While a reasonably energetic backpacker may walk 15 or 20 miles in a day, the equivalent distance for a cyclist is probably between 75 and 100 miles. Both friction that must be constantly overcome and the work of going up and down the inevitable hills are significantly greater with increased weight. That's why racers and many other serious cyclists work hard and pay a lot of money to shave just a couple of pounds— or even ounces—from their bicycles. A pound in your panniers is just as hard to move up a grade as the same weight in the frame. This isn't to say that you can't enjoy cycle camping with less than perfect equipment. The addition of weight slows you down a good deal, however.

Choose whatever equipment you carry for cycling camping with care. Learn to take a minimum of extra clothing. If you're concerned with fashion, then buy some stylish cycling clothes that you won't be ashamed to wear when you get off the bike. Camping gear for cycling trips can usually be fairly light, because you rarely go on bike trips during those times of year when severe weather is the rule.

Of course, you may have to compromise a little on weight to use equipment you already possess for other activities, but if cycling is one of the things you're planning when you buy gear, try to keep it as light as possible. A double sleeping-bag system for cold weather would make a lot of sense if you were also thinking about cycle camping, since half of the system would be adequate for most bicycle tours. Unless you can afford an ultralight tent, a tube tent, tarp, or a fly from a mountain tent is a good shelter for many bike trips.

Figure 40 Bicycle camping is a fine way to enjoy the countryside. Travel is fast enough to allow the cyclist to cover a lot of ground but slow enough so that he or she can enjoy the surroundings. In country like this, it's easy to find a campsite when you're ready to stop.

You should try to plan meals so that as little weight as possible has to be carried along from day to day. Seasonings and the like are usually carried for the whole trip, of course, but except in fairly remote spots, it's rarely necessary to carry more than a couple of days' food supply at a time. Often you can stop to pick up lunch items at a store late in the morning, and supper and breakfast food in the afternoon.

THE BIKE

It would be impossible to go into any detail about the design of touring bikes in the space available here. Anyone planning to purchase an expensive bicycle should do a good deal of research and shopping around to find out what's available. The now-familiar ten-speed bicycle is standard for good reason, although there are arguments in favor of three-speed touring bikes for regions that aren't too hilly. In any event, the serious bicycle tourer wants a reasonably well-made bicycle. Nearly all three-speeds sold in this country and a lot of ten-speeds are heavy and weak. They'll do for an introduction to the sport, but the beginner should recognize their limitations.

It is best to have a fairly narrow seat and dropped handlebars on a bike intended for long-distance touring. A wide saddle with coil springs may feel comfortable for riding around town, but after 25 miles or so, its disadvantages become all too apparent. Dropped handlebars permit a variety of positions for the hands and body, as well as being more efficient for hard pedaling.

Good-quality components on the touring bike are well worthwhile, both in terms of weight and durability. Decent brakes are critical for safety. The importance of a strong frame and fork may not be so obvious to beginners, but a little thought given to the consequences of breakage during a high-speed downhill ride should be convincing. Touring frames are generally made a bit longer and somewhat less stiff than racing frames. Most people prefer wider gear ranges than those used for racing, and rear wheels should be fairly strong, since they'll carry the weight of panniers as well as that of rider and cycle. Sealed bearings are particularly useful to the tourer, since roadside cleaning of bearings and their races is a nuisance.

Opinion is divided as to what sort of tires are best for touring. *Sew-ups* (tubulars) are light, and weight on the wheel is far more critical than weight anywhere else, because it has to be accelerated far more than any other part of the bike. On the other hand, sew-ups are fragile, expensive, and difficult to repair. *Clinchers,* or tires made like those of automobiles, are preferred by an increasing number of cycle tourists because of their lower cost and the simplicity of repairing them. Lighter-weight clinchers are available these days, including some that can be looped into a compact bundle for carrying as spare.

Heavier clinchers should be used on the roads where punctures are very likely. Sew-ups are literally sewn together along their inside diameter, so that the tire forms a closed tube around the inner tube. The tire is glued to a shallow groove in the rim. A repair requires opening the stitches, patching, restitching, and regluing. Clinchers are open along the inside circumference. Each edge has a wire embedded in the rubber, and the wires hold the tire in place on a deeply grooved rim. A tube can be repaired by simply removing the tire and patching it. Whatever tires are chosen, they should be inflatable to quite high pressures. High-pressure tires have far less rolling resistance than those not inflated so strongly.

SPECIAL EQUIPMENT

Most of the specialized gear important for bicycle campers has been discussed in preceding chapters, particularly those on packs, clothing, and footwear. The bicycle itself is, of course, the most important additional item for cycling. There are a few other things that should be mentioned, though.

Careful consideration must be given in advance to the problem of protecting the bicycle when it's left unattended. The cyclist has to decide whether or not to carry a lock and a chain or cable, and if so, how heavy it should be. On some trips, one can rely on staying close to the bike, on leaving it in a safe place, or on concealing it. In other situations a lightweight protective device to discourage a casual thief may be adequate. Sometimes nothing but a heavy, hardened chain and lock stands any chance of securing a cycle against theft. This is a serious problem, since the chains needed in areas where theft is a major threat are likely to be heavier than the bicycle they are made to protect.

On most camping trips, the risk isn't really major one,

and a light chain is the most that's needed. If you stop at a commercial establishment and the bikes can't be kept within view, ask for a safe place to store them. Visiting areas where you want to hike around and where thieves are active can present particular difficulties. If destinations like national parks are involved, you may be able to call or write ahead and ask if there's a safe storage place. There should be something available in popular and heavily visited areas; locking racks which require only a coin deposit or a lock, not a whole chain, can be provided. In any case, you may be able to plan in advance. Paying a small fee to the operator of a store or gas station to keep the bikes safe may sometimes save you the difficulty of carrying a heavy chain. When traveling in a group, work out the lightest combination of chains to protect all the bikes.

Tool kits also should be carried on all but the shortest bicycles trips. Think out your tool kit well in advance, and put together the lightest one that will take care of common difficulties. Read a bike-repair manual or two, learn to do your own maintenance work, and you'll be ready to handle minor problems on the road. Don't forget to carry spare spokes, tire-repair kits, and a pump. Specialized tools, such as freewheel removers and crank tools, may be particularly important, since there's no way they can be borrowed from a friendly gas-station attendant.

Lights need calls for the special attention of cyclists, whose needs are somewhat different from those of other campers. Three considerations have to be borne in mind when choosing lights for cycle camping: using them in camp, lighting your own way on dark roads, and making yourself visible to motorists. Even if you don't plan to ride after dark, it's usually prudent to allow for unforeseen difficulties. Reflective tape can be used as a lightweight and effective alternative to other reflectors. It can be put on the backs of pedals, seat tubes, fenders, panniers, clothing, and light plastic strips to be laced through the spokes for riding in the dark, while stored in the panniers the rest of the time. The small leg lights that operate on two C-cells can be effective in attracting the motorist's eye and can be used if necessary for camp lights.

Generator-driven lights are preferred by many to provide a view of the road. They save the expense of batteries and the worry about their wearing out just when they're needed. On the other hand, generator setups are costly at the start, weigh a lot, can't be used as camp lights, and don't operate when you stop to look at a sign or wait at an intersection. Battery-operated lamps mounted on the bike may be used; they should be removable for use in camp. Headlamps can also be used effectively for cycling at night, and they make excellent lights in camp, because they leave the hands free for cooking, setting up a tent, or unpacking duffel.

A helmet to protect the head in the event of an accident should be given serious consideration by the touring cyclist. Ideally, it should be light, comfortable, and well ventilated. It should also provide good head protection, unlike the padded strips of leather typically worn by racers. The helmets made by Bell and MSR are particularly good.

chapter
17

Ski Touring And Snowshoeing

There are some special pleasures in extending lightweight camping into the winter months, especially in those regions that receive a lot of snow. The crowds are far smaller, even in popular areas, once you're a few miles away from the road. The woods and the mountains take on a new beauty when they're covered with snow and ice, and the very harshness of the surroundings makes winter trips particularly rewarding.

If the snow isn't very deep, then walking tours can be taken just about the same way they are in the summer, except that equipment has to be suited to the more difficult climatic conditions. Footwear, in particular, has to be adequate for protection, and gaiters are essential to keep snow out of the boots. With a deep enough snow cover, however, it becomes virtually impossible to move at all without something to spread the weight of the body and pack out enough to hold you on top of the snow. Keep in mind that in snowy regions a storm can change the snow cover from one in which walking is feasible to one that's waist deep. The storm may well come when you're a dozen miles from the nearest road.

Figure 41 Winter travel is particularly satisfying and beautiful, but the conditions can be harsh, and careful preparation is important. Here a snowshoer crosses a windswept frozen lake.

Either skis or snowshoes provide good means of traveling over snow. Each method has certain advantages over the other, and each has strong partisans. Snowshoes tend to be more suitable where there's a lot of brush through which you have to pick a path and where the snow isn't deep enough to cover most of the rocks, small brush, and forest deadfall that are encountered along the easiest path. With only a moderate amount of snow, skis may be suitable for traveling along snow-covered roads and trails, while snowshoes are needed for beating your way cross-country. Snowshoes are also more compact and, therefore, easier to carry when they're not in use. They're quite easy to learn to use, require no special footwear, and tend to be somewhat cheaper than skis. Skis usually permit faster travel and are more enjoyable when worn by a competent skier, at least when the snow is sufficiently deep to smooth over surface obstacles.

BEGINNING WINTER CAMPING

Camping in real winter conditions—in deep snow and cold weather—is generally a good deal more strenuous than living outdoors at other times of the year. You must pay more careful attention to equipment, because you must rely more on it. Often more things have to be carried, and winter clothing must be worn. The combination of thick clothing, a heavy pack, cold temperatures, and the hard work of breaking trail through fresh snow causes a lot of problems with wet clothing due to perspiration and condensation. If moisture is also added by wet snow, the winter traveler is constantly plagued by difficulties with damp clothes. A lot of attention must be given to keeping clothes dry; the techniques eventually become automatic, but the beginner has to take great care to keep things as dry as possible. This is also the reason why wool, acrylic-pile, and polyester insulated clothing are favorites in the winter. They retain some insulating capacity when wet, and they dry quickly.

There are enough extra complications in winter camping, at least when conditions are difficult, that it's important not to deal with too many of them at the same time. Go out on a day hike or two on snowshoes before heading out on a ten-mile walk with a heavy pack and camp to set up at the end of the day. Ski-touring technique *must* be learned fairly well before you attempt to go out with a large pack and a lot of brand-new winter gear that you've never even tried. Spend your first night out on the snow close to the road, so that you have plenty of time to learn to make a winter camp and can bail out if problems arise.

Safety margins are much smaller in winter than in summer. Traveling is usually a lot more strenuous, packs are heavy, days are short, and everything tends to be very time-consuming. The combination of exhaustion, wet clothes, and a cold wind can sap energy reserves very rapidly. On their first few trips, people may get dangerously cold very quickly. Young people and thin people are particularly prone to rapid chilling, because they have larger surface areas from which to lose heat for their weights, and because they have less insulating fat. People who aren't in good physical condition are also particularly vulnerable.

The point is simply to take things slowly when first beginning to camp in the winter. Add a few problems with each trip, and you'll soon be able to camp with the same assurance and safety that you do in the summer. If you learn to build snow shelters, you may even be able to get your pack down to the same weight as a summer one.

SNOWSHOES

Snowshoes come in a large number of designs, made from a variety of materials. Size is one of the main choices you must make and one of the clearest. The bigger the area of each shoe, the less it will sink into soft snow before supporting your weight. Less sinking means less effort expended to climb up out of each step, but this has to be balanced against the effort of lifting and maneuvering large shoes. Bigger people with heavier packs need larger snowshoes for the same flotation in snow. Smaller snowshoes are often carried for occasional or emergency use, as when you're backpacking in the fall when the first big storm may arrive anytime. Larger shoes are required for flotation in regions with soft, deep snow.

Shapes are also quite varied. The shoes should fit together when you're striding along, so that a very wide gait isn't required. In general, shorter tailless snowshoes are more maneuverable and easier to handle in deadfall, brush, and rocks. Tails help in swinging the snowshoes straight ahead without a lot of snow drag against the rear. Long snowshoes are useful for rapid going on trails that aren't too steep. Mountaineers prefer narrow snowshoes that will allow edging on slopes of soft snow. Steep, hard snow requires some kind of cleat under the foot. Bindings that give a lot of control are also important on difficult terrain.

Materials for snowshoes have undergone many changes in the last few years. Wooden shoes laced with rawhide are traditional. They work well, but they must be revarnished periodically to prevent water soaking in from wet snow. Neoprene-coated nylon material is superior to rawhide if it's of good quality. It may be strung on wood frames or aluminum ones. The lightest and strongest snowshoes currently available are made from aluminum tubing with membranes of neoprene-nylon. Keep in mind that any of these materials can be used to make bad snowshoes as well as good ones. Plastic snowshoes have been made with some success, but they're heavy for their size and strength compared with some other materials, and they haven't always held up under heavy use. Their main advantage is price. They're fine for occasional use. Fiberglass-like materials have been used with some success, but no commercially manufactured models are currently available.

SKI TOURING

Ski touring has been one of the fastest growing of all outdoor activities in the past five years or so. Not long ago, hardly any lightweight touring skis were even imported into North America. Now there are not only hundreds of thousands of pairs imported but also at least a half-dozen American manufacturers. Ski touring can be enjoyed at widely varying levels of difficulty, both in terms of distance traveled and steepness of terrain covered. Although downhill skiing experience speeds learning of touring technique somewhat, it's not at all necessary. Touring can be self-taught without much difficulty, although some people prefer to take lessons. You should plan to go out and do quite a bit of day touring before undertaking long overnight trips. Of course, you can always set up camp near a road and tour from your camp, particularly if you don't live close to a good touring area. The important point is that you'll neither enjoy yourself nor learn to ski well if you're fighting constantly with a heavy pack.

It would be completely impossible to discuss all the equipment that's available to the ski tourer these days. There's a complete range of weight, durability, and control from cross-country racing skis, weighing less than three pounds a pair with bindings, to heavy alpine skis, which may weigh fifteen pounds. In

Figure 42 Provided there's sufficient snow cover, the cross-country skier can move faster and have much more fun than the snowshoer, but linked telemark turns like this one require practice, particularly when skiing with a heavy pack.

general, a ski tourer looking for one pair of skis that will serve well for general touring and winter camping should obtain a pair of standard touring or light touring skis with Nordic three-pin bindings. The better grades of skis using synthetic materials or laminations of fiberglass and wood are more durable than traditional wood skis, and are therefore more suitable for back-country use. Synthetic bottoms have been much improved in the past few years, and they now hold cross-country waxes quite well if they're properly prepared.

Most experienced ski tourers still prefer to use cross-country waxes to give them traction in normal snow conditions. Such waxes are designed to provide a good grip on the snow for the ski that's planted solidly but to glide well once the ski is moving. To provide both characteristics, the wax must be of just the right hardness for the conditions encountered, and learning to wax skis properly is one of the tricks that the beginning cross-country skier needs to learn. Proper waxing is very important, too, for the snow camper, because climbing a slope with a heavy pack can be exhausting if the skis either slip backward or pick up heavy clumps of snow. In some circumstances, there are advantages to *no-wax bottoms*, which consist of either indentations in the bottom or strips of mohair glued into grooves near the center of the ski. In either case the idea is to permit the ski to slide forward freely, while preventing it from sliding backward. Ski mountaineers often use *climbers* or *skins*, which fasten to the bottoms of the skis and permit climbing much steeper slopes than can be managed with waxes.

SNOW CAMPING

A few special aspects of camping in the snow are particularly worth mentioning. Water is often not available in liquid form, so that it has to be melted from snow or ice. Fuel requirements are doubled as a result, and stoves with a high heat output have great advantages. Condensation problems inside tents are much worse because of cold outside temperatures, moisture that's accumulated in equipment, and vapor from cooking inside the tent. Special care must be taken to provide good ventilation if it's necessary to cook inside, because stoves use a lot of oxygen and frequently produce significant quantities of carbon monoxide. Quite a few items may have to be taken into the sleeping bag to prevent them from freezing: water bottles, fuel canisters for butane and propane stoves, and boots.

Special attention should be paid to footwear for winter use. Boots shouldn't be too tight, since restriction of circulation is one cause of cold feet. Stiff boots should be used only if absolutely necessary. Special warm footwear for use around camp is worth considering, particularly for ski tourers using lightweight boots or climbers using stiff ones. Overboots of some kind are another option. There are various kinds made for climbers, including some that leave the sole exposed, and there are special foam-insulated overboots made to go over ski touring boots and to work with pin bindings.

Campers using tents should either carry wide stakes suitable for use in snow or attach extra lengths of line to stake loops. These lines can be tied around sticks or rocks which can then be buried in the snow and stamped down. In deep snow a platform for the tent has to be packed and then allowed to harden before pitching the tent.

Experienced winter campers prefer snow shelters to tents in many situations. There are many kinds, each with certain advantages. The most familiar type is the igloo, a dome-shaped shelter constructed with blocks cut from consolidated snow. However, snow caves dug in drifted snow, hollows under snow-covered trees, trenches covered over with tarps or snow blocks, and a dozen different sorts of hybrid structures may be more suitable in a particular situation. Snow conditions and the terrain tend to determine which sort of structure is best. Snow shelters are much warmer than tents, because they're completely

Figure 43 A snowshoer with a nearly completed snow shelter, far warmer than a tent. This shelter is a hybrid of a cave and an igloo. The best snow shelter for a particular occasion is often dictated by conditions, and practice is essential before the camper can depend on building one. Some igloos can be seen in the photograph in Figure 12.

protected from the wind and because snow itself is a good insulator. The savings in weight and bulk are significant also, since campers using snow shelters needn't carry tents and can often be comfortable with lighter sleeping bags; they need only a few tools like shovels and block-cutting implements.

There's no substitute for experience in learning to build snow shelters. The first few attempts are always very time-consuming, and the participants usually get quite wet wallowing around in the snow. It isn't advisable to go out on a long trip and plan on camping in a snow shelter without plenty of practice beforehand. Experienced builders of caves, trenches, and igloos can often construct shelters faster than tentsites can be prepared, however. With a suitable snowdrift, a practiced camper can dig a good one-person snow cave in 15 or 20 minutes, with the additional advantage that after the first five minutes, he or she is protected from the wind.

HAZARDS

Two particular hazards should be mentioned in connection with winter camping: hypothermia and avalanches. Hypothermia (chilling of the body core) is discussed briefly in Chapter XIII, and cold weather travelers must pay special heed to symptoms. Inexperienced people are especially vulnerable to hypothermia, because they're less familiar with their capacities and are less likely to recognize the warning signs when they begin to get into difficulty. For most people it's very important to stop frequently for a little food, so that blood sugar for immediate energy isn't depleted. It's also important to maintain adequate fluid intake. Dehydration is common in winter, when you're perspiring and breathing hard in dry air. Put on warm clothing as soon as you stop for a rest, and shed before you start sweating again. Watch for signs of hypothermia in yourself and your companions. A pale face or a bluish tint in the lips or fingernails is one sign. Despondency, irrationality, refusal to eat or put on warm clothes are all typical signs. A person just getting cold needs to be protected from the wind, warmed, and given rest and food. More serious cases require active rewarming by another person in a sleeping bag under shelter.

Avalanches are another hazard that must be considered by winter travelers in mountainous areas. Any snow slope steeper than about 25° is a likely avalanche run unless the snow is anchored by heavy timber. Scattered trees don't make a slope safe. Long experience is needed to judge the stability of snow, though avalanches are most likely to occur after a heavy

206 SELF-PROPELLED TRAVEL—AN INTRODUCTION

snow or rapid deposition of snow by wind. If you travel in mountainous terrain in the winter, learn all you can about avalanche forecasting and precautions, and until you're an expert, stay away from potential avalanche slopes. Remember that small avalanches may still bury a snowshoer or ski tourer. When in doubt, stay off steep slopes.

chapter 18 | **Mountaineering And Climbing**

Mountaineering and its offshoots, like rock climbing, are some of the most exciting and challenging of all outdoor activities. Among the high peaks and spires, the climber can experience the most profound joys of the human encounter with nature. I hesitate to write briefly about climbing technique, however, because the skills and equipment needed for many mountaineering activities are specialized, subtle, and complex. Climbing may be either dangerous or safe when practiced by experienced mountaineers, and one of the greatest difficulties for the novice is developing an understanding of what he or she can undertake safely. Climbing can be extremely hazardous for eager beginners whose ambitions outrun their abilities.

Most of the activities described in this book are inherently safe. With reasonable prudence and common sense, serious accidents can be almost completely avoided, and there's no reason why you must enlist the help of an expert to learn backpacking, bicycle camping, or ski touring. Climbing is something else again. Anyone who wants to learn to do difficult climbs quickly without taking a lot of severe risks had better find an experienced mentor. Any form of self-instruction is likely to be slow, dangerous, or both. Some good books on climbing are listed in the appendix, but even studying of these only familiarizes the aspiring climber with the standard techniques used in the sport; real understanding develops only with experience.

A great deal of mountaineering can be regarded as simply an offshoot of backpacking or hiking, and this sort of climbing can be enjoyable in itself, as well as a safe introduction to harder routes. Most of the mountains in the United States aren't precipitous or fearsome, and climbing them simply involves walking up, perhaps following a trail or scrambling up rock fields. The only differences between hiking up a mountain of this sort and taking any other backcountry excursion are that the weather is likely to be more severe if it deteriorates and that finding your way may be trickier. The experienced hiker and backpacker will discover that still other peaks involve easy clambering on rocks, which is harder than hiking but not too difficult for an experienced wilderness traveler. There's no really clear demarcation line between such moderate scrambling and *technical mountaineering*, climbing that requires the use of ropes and related equipment to provide a reasonable margin of safety. Indeed, the border is often crossed when the weather changes, as when a little freezing rain changes a hikers' route to one suitable only for skilled mountaineers.

One of the hazy areas between serious mountaineering and hiking is found on snow slopes, which provide easy access to many peaks, particularly in the spring and early summer when they're consolidated enough to hold the walker up but still soft enough so that steps are easily stamped in the surface. A little practice rapidly generates enough confidence to convince a hiker of the ease with which such slopes can be climbed. It's important to recognize several hazards associated with them, however. Warming by sun, wind, or rain can cause avalanches, and these are particularly common early in the year from midmorning until the sun has left the slopes in the afternoon or evening.

A second hazard is simply that of slipping and sliding to the bottom. Even a slope that's easy to ascend may be quite steep enough to accelerate a fall to dangerous velocity. The harder the snow is, the more rapidly a misstep turns into a terrifying slide. The danger is particularly great if the slope gets steeper below or if there are rocks or cliffs at the bottom. Mountaineers use ice axes to safeguard themselves against slips on moderate snow slopes. The pick of the ax can be driven into the snow and used as a brake, a technique known as self-arrest. The method can be self-taught by studying one of the mountaineering books mentioned in the appendix and going out and practicing on a safe slope. Knowledge of self-arrest technique can greatly extend a hiker's and backpacker's range in the mountains. It's important to realize that there's no substitute for thorough practice of self-arrests; simply knowing how they are done is worthless. The muscles must be trained to perform the arrest as a reflex action.

The third point which should be noted regarding moderate snow slopes is that they are generally much harder to descend than to climb. Psychologically, a slope which appears quite manageable when one is looking into the incline and beginning at the bottom is likely to be terrifying when regarded from the top looking down. The technique of climbing down, usually by facing out and driving the heels in with plunging steps, is also more difficult. Finally, snow slopes change during the day, and in a few hours one that's easy to ascend may turn into either an avalanche trap or an icy ramp. Beware of going up something you may not be able to get back down.

TECHNICAL CLIMBING

Technical climbing, whether on rock, snow, ice, or all three, is climbing that normally requires a rope and other specialized techniques for reasonable safety. By far the best way to learn technical climbing is to get a friend who is a competent climber to take you out and teach you. A second efficient method is to search out a good climbing school or a guide service that offers instructional programs. Clubs often run climbing schools taught by good instructors for a nominal fee. Your progress will be speeded and you'll waste less time if you read all you can beforehand, but self-instruction is by far the least desirable method of learning to climb. Progress is too slow, and there are dozens of pitfalls to trap the unwary. There's a lot that can be learned with no help, though, both from books and from activities other than serious climbing. Backpacking and scrambling around the high country teach the novice a lot of the things the mountaineer needs to know, from weather lore to balancing while hopping across a talus field with a pack. If you can find a small rock outcrop near home, you can also get a lot of worthwhile practice climbing around the base a few feet from the ground, making the most difficult moves you can. You may also meet experienced climbers during such '"bouldering" sessions.

Figure 44 Technical climbing on rock can be one of the most enjoyable of outdoor activities for those who appreciate challenge and difficulty, as well as the beauty of nature. This is a free climb, and the nuts hanging from the climber's hardware loop are used only for protection against a fall, not to make progress.

When two climbers undertake a route that's difficult enough to pose a significant danger of falling and high enough, that the consequences would be disastrous, they normally tie themselves together with a *climbing rope.* The majority of climbing ropes in use in North America are 150 feet long and 11 millimeters (7/16 inch) in diameter. Modern materials and rope handling techniques are at the heart of the advances in climbing standards that have occurred since the World War II. The nylon ropes in use today for climbing absorb the impact of the most severe falls without either breaking or putting intolerable stress on the climber's body. Though it's still not advisable to fall, except in practice situations, a leader who does can be stopped and usually escapes severe injury. In an earlier era, a bad fall by the leader normally was fatal.

The rope alone is used on climbs that are difficult enough for a slip to carry one of the climbers off a cliff or perhaps into a crevasse on a glacier. On difficult vertical terrain, however, a whole arsenal of associated equipment is used in combination with the rope to safeguard the climbers. Central to roped climbing technique is *belaying.* Only one climber moves at a time, and the second person is tied firmly to the mountain. The nonclimbing partner belays the rope by passing it around his or her body or through a friction device so that the grip of one hand, usually gloved, is sufficient to arrest a fall. As the leader moves up, various pieces of nylon rope or webbing (slings) and metal devices are used to attach the rope to the mountain. Such attachments are made through *carabiners,* oval rings, each of which has a spring-loaded gate in one side, so that the rope is held to attachment points but can slide freely. If the leader falls, she or he drops only twice the distance from the last anchor before the rope comes taut and begins to stop the tumble.

The beginner should get a lot of advance practice in belaying before using the technique to protect real climbs. Once the motions have been mastered, there is no substitute for using the method to arrest the fall of a heavy weight dropped from some distance. This can be done by throwing a weight over a local cliff, to be caught by a well-anchored belayer sitting above, starting with a few feet of slack in the rope, and working up to 30 feet or so. Climbing schools often use a tower with pulley arrangements to substitute for the cliff. If the weight is comparable to that of a climber, the belayer will develop a realistic appreciation of the forces involved in a fall.

These techniques and others have made many sorts of climbing relatively safe—which is not to say easy—for competent practitioners. Some kinds of mountaineering and climbing have high inherent risks, however, and the differences aren't always apparent to the beginner. There are also many climbs that can be undertaken with little risk by very good climbers but that involve severe hazards for those only moderately skilled. Falling rock may be a hazard on many routes, particularly in the high mountains, so considerable care, good climbing technique, and judgment are needed to prevent injuries. Weather can be a serious danger among the peaks, where a sudden storm may catch the unwary in the middle of a difficult face, icing the rocks and creating avalanche hazards in snow chutes. Lightning is a major danger if climbers are caught by thunderstorms. Convenient spots where anchors can be attached to the mountain aren't always available, though the ingenuity of equipment manufacturers constantly improves the possibilities.

Climbing itself has a number of more specialized subdivisions, some of which are mentioned briefly here in the following paragraphs. In fact, alpine skiing was once a branch of mountaineering, though it's now an almost completely separate sport.

Rock climbing is what most people think about when climbing is mentioned at all. Besides the steep faces of mountains, there are cliffs, rock outcroppings, and canyon walls all over the country where good rock climbing can be found. Rock climbing is enjoyable in itself at almost any level of difficulty, and it provides excellent training for all sorts of technical climbing. Weather problems, long approaches, and many other problems are often eliminated from rock climbing, which is frequently done on sunny local cliffs a few hundred feet high. If the weather turns bad or a climb proves too difficult, it's a relatively simple matter to get off and go home. The techniques of placing protection, belaying, and climbing can be worked on and perfected readily, and those techniques can then be extended to big rock walls and mountain faces. Rock climbing centers, particularly at Yosemite Valley in California, have been responsible for most advances in American climbing.

Rock climbers generally wear harnesses made of nylon webbing around their waists and thighs, to absorb the force of a fall. Protection is obtained by looping slings over projections of rock or by inserting blocks of metal, usually aluminum, into wide sections of cracks or pockets, in such a way that a fall would jam them tightly into a narrower part of the crack. These metal pieces, made in various shapes and known as *nuts* or *chocks,* are threaded with nylon or cable slings to which a longer sling or a carabiner can be attached. They don't mar the rock as the pitons that were formerly used do. (Pitons are metal wedges driven into cracks with hammers.) Climbers may wear helmets to protect their heads both from falling rock and from injury in a fall.

Most rock climbing is *free climbing,* and the ropes and hardware are used only to protect the climbers against the possibility of a fall, not for aiding their progress. Some climbs, particularly on very large and smooth vertical rock faces, are accomplished by actually hanging from nuts or other hardware and using them for progress. This is called *aid climbing.* In general, this technique is avoided when a climb can be done without it.

Snow climbing can range from easy plodding up snow slopes, in which steps can be easily kicked, to quite steep and difficult going on severe faces. It may include climbing on tumbled glaciers on peaks in Canada, Alaska, and the Pacific Northwest. Protection on moderate snow climbs is furnished by self-arrest. Roped climbing may be protected by belays from

Figure 45 Aid climbing. The climber in this photograph is using nuts in the cracks of the overhanging rock to climb on, by attaching short ladders made of nylon webbing, but when he moves up another foot or so he will start free climbing. Direct aid is used as little as possible. Difficulty ranges widely from easy walking to strenuous and athletic climbing.

ice axes driven into the snow or specially designed aluminum plates called snow flukes. Snow climbs change more than rock climbs, according to snow condition, and protection may be difficult to obtain on hard climbs. Compacted snow and snow that has alternately melted and frozen for some time begin to turn into ice, so there's no clear dividing line between snow and ice climbing. For ice and hard snow, the climber uses *crampons,* metal frames that are provided with sharp spikes protruding down and forward to grip the snow or ice and that are strapped onto the boots.

Ice climbing, although it's sometimes similar to snow

climbing and is most frequently done in the high mountains, may also take place on frozen waterfalls, just as rock climbing is often done on local cliffs. New ice-climbing implements and techniques have permitted climbers to tackle more severe routes in the last few years. On very steep ice the climber typically uses rigid crampons with front points projecting out ahead of the toes and an ice ax and hammer, each of which has a drooped pick that sticks in the ice without popping out when pulled on. Protection is gained either from nearby rock or from special *ice screws* placed in the ice itself. Ice climbing tends to be less safe and less easily protected than rock climbing, with the margin of safety depending more on the skill of the climber than on equipment.

General mountaineering may range from easy roped climbing, only a bit harder than the hiker's scrambling, to ascending very severe routes that demand the greatest proficiency in all the specialties of rock, snow, and ice climbing. The mountaineer often has to move faster and with less equipment than in climbing of similar difficulty on rocks near home. Heavy mountain boots must be used if a route involves snow and ice, whereas lightweight, tight-fitting rock shoes are frequently worn on pure rock climbs. Problems of weather and long approaches are more common. The mountaineer moving back and forth among snow, rock, and ice may have to chop steps in ice pitches or wear crampons while rock climbing. The general mountaineer who undertakes difficult routes must be proficient in all the climbing specialties.

Climbing is one of the most esthetic and challenging of wilderness arts. It offers its devotees the most sublime experiences of the forces of nature as well as days of fun in the sun. However, it's well to remind yourself occasionally of the words of Edward Whymper, who led the first ascent of the Matterhorn over a century ago and watched four of his companions fall to their deaths during the descent. He wrote, "There have been joys too great to be described in words, and there have been griefs upon which I have not dared to dwell; and with these in mind I say, climb if you will, but remember that courage and strength are nought without prudence, and that a momentary negligence may destroy the happiness of a lifetime. Do nothing in haste; look well to each step; and from the beginning think what may be the end."

chapter 19 | Canoeing

The canoe is perhaps the most marvelous and certainly the most versatile of small watercraft. A properly made canoe is rugged, can be carried by one person even over difficult terrain, is maneuverable enough to be guided through intricate boulder gardens, is rugged enough to withstand hard use, has such a shallow draft it can be paddled or poled in a few inches of water, is sufficiently seaworthy to be used in large waves and rapids of considerable difficulty, and carries enough weight through the water gracefully to keep the lightweight traveler self-sufficient for long periods.

A canoe can be used for an afternoon with the family on a pond in a city park or a month-long journey down a remote river north of the Arctic Circle. It makes travel pleasant and relatively easy in many wilderness areas that are almost impenetrable on foot. Its near perfection for backcountry travel in many parts of North America explains why this Indian invention has been improved only slightly in hundreds of years. It is a model of the proper relationship between form and function.

The choice of a canoe is too large a subject to consider in detail here. A new boat costs between $200 and $600 at the

Figure 46 The canoe is the entrée to tens of thousands of lakes and other waterways that speckle the continent. Some of the most beautiful wilderness in North America can be reached in no other way.

time this is written, so it's not a trivial investment for most people. There are more bad canoes on the market than good ones, particularly if you're judging by the standards of the wilderness trekker. Versatile as they are, canoes must be designed as compromises, like most equipment suited for the backcountry. The maneuverability that's desirable for the white-water paddler isn't wholly compatible with the ability to hold a course well, which is needed by the canoeist working across a large lake. Light weight must be balanced to some degree against durability and carrying capacity.

For the wilderness canoeist, there are currently three boat materials that should normally be considered: aluminum, thermoplastics like ABS, and laminates of resin with fiberglass and similar materials. All these are currently employed by various manufacturers to make superb wilderness canoes. Wood-and-canvas construction, though it's esthetically pleasing, has been largely supplanted by these modern materials, for good reasons.

Check the models available in your area or in places you may visit before buying a canoe. (Shipping costs are outrageous.) Try to rent and borrow canoes, and learn to paddle before you buy, if possible. Consider what you want the canoe to do, what sacrifices you're willing to make, and what you plan to use the boat for. Talk to as many experienced canoeists as you can find, and read some books on the subject. As a general rule, try to avoid the seeming attractions of a canoe that's touted as wide, very stable, and impossible to tip over. A barge has all these characteristics, but it doesn't paddle well. Within limits, the stability of a canoe is provided by the paddlers, not by a wide beam and flat bottom.

The paddle is as important as the canoe. Without it the canoeist is helpless: it provides the means of pushing the boat through the water and much of the stability that may be needed in rough water. Weight and feel are important, since the canoeist on a trip dips his or her paddle into the water many thousands of times in a day. Good wood paddles are the standard against which others are judged, and the best ones are made of carefully laminated wood. However, fiberglass-bladed paddles are tougher and usually less expensive than wooden ones of the same quality. Shafts may be of fiberglass or plastic-covered aluminum. A good paddle should be light and durable and should feel springy when the blade is rested on the floor and the shaft is weighted. The blade should be of suitable size: eight inches is a typical width. As for length, a paddle reaching from floor to chin works fairly well. Spare paddles are essential for wilderness travel.

A pole is also a good implement to propel a canoe, and the advent of modern aluminum poles has revolutionized the art of poling. The technique of poling can't be described here; the interested reader should check the books mentioned in the appendix.

LEARNING TO PADDLE

Learning to paddle a canoe is mostly a matter of practice. Get a book that describes the basic strokes and principles of guiding the boat, and then go out on a lake. You should be a good swimmer before you begin, of course, and particularly when you're starting, it's important to observe proper safety precautions. Go out on calm water when the wind isn't blowing, stay near shore and away from power craft, and wear a wet suit before venturing any distance over water that's cold. Wear a life preserver at all times until you know what you're doing and when it's cool or you're around white water.

Whether you paddle in tandem, which is easier than working alone, or by yourself, you may find your first few experiences a little frustrating. A good canoe is sensitive to the paddle, and this means that it may go in every direction except the one you intend until you've mastered the basic strokes. The most important is the J-stroke, which is used by the lone paddler or the stern person to keep the canoe from being turned away from the paddling side. In the J-stroke, a straight stroke is made to drive the canoe forward, and the paddle is turned and pushed outward slightly just at the end of the stroke. Learn to keep the canoe on course without changing paddling sides. You shouldn't *have* to switch to make the boat go where you want it to.

Paddling the canoe around a lake becomes second nature fairly soon. Spend some time learning to maneuver around buoys or other convenient obstacles, and you will gain a reasonable facility rather quickly. This is all the ability that's needed for many easy canoe-camping trips. In fact, it's all the ability that most people who paddle ever attain. To achieve real competence in handling a canoe, however, a lot more practice is required, preferably under the guidance of a really experienced paddler. Handling a canoe in large waves on a windy lake or in even the easiest of rapids is a world away from paddling through lily pads in calm weather. More difficult canoeing isn't everyone's cup of tea, but it's important to at least recognize your own limitations. Until you've acquired the necessary skills, don't go out when the wind is up, don't go very far from shore in large lakes or bays, and don't venture onto any but the calmest rivers, where you *know* exactly what's downstream. Paddling in even an easy current is quite different from guiding the canoe on a lake.

River canoeing often demands a sophisticated understanding of the dynamics of flowing water and its effects on the hull of the boat. Paddling confidently on large waves and in white water requires advanced strokes in which the canoeist uses the paddle to brace against the surface of the water, tapping the power of opposing currents to maneuver the canoe. There's no substitute for carefully acquired experience in handling difficult water. A stretch of rapids that would not even catch the attention of an experienced river canoeist may spell disaster for the novice. Difficult paddling often requires several boats for safety as well, but there's safety in numbers only if the level of competence of the whole party is adequate to the circumstances.

The ease of carrying a canoe around most rapids is one of the features that makes it a good wilderness craft, and it's also what enables many canoeists of intermediate level to negotiate rivers that may contain difficult rapids. One of the first skills of the wilderness canoeist is that of pulling in to shore and scouting the river ahead. The beginning river paddler must learn at an early stage how to judge the speed of the current and to get across it to a landing as quickly as possible. The experienced boater never runs a section willingly beyond a point where he or she can pull out. The mystery of what's around the next bend is the spice of life to the canoeist, but one that shouldn't be tasted without an advance look.

CANOE CAMPING

Of all lightweight campers, the canoeist is perhaps the freest from the constrictions of weight. At least on easy lake trips of only a few days' duration, the addition of 10 or 15 pounds is of little consequence. For this same reason, the canoeist can often manage longer treks without resupply than any other wilderness traveler. Many canoes 17 or 18 feet long can carry several hundred pounds in addition to two paddlers. Weight isn't a negligible consideration, but the canoeist is far less restricted than the backpacker or cyclist.

The other special characteristics of canoe camping relate mainly to constant proximity to water. Rainwear and shelter while camping tend to be important to canoe campers because good canoeing country usually receives a large amount of precipitation. Dry footwear for use on land is almost always carried, since it's often necessary to wade in the water when launching or landing a boat, and marshy areas that have to be crossed are common. Water splashing into the bottom of the boat may be a familiar part of many trips as well.

Extremely cold temperatures are rare on canoe trips, so sleeping bags don't have to be very thick, but it's important to keep them dry. Sleeping bags, extra clothing, and food that would be damaged by water must be packed in dry packs or sealed inside several layers of plastic bags. Polyester-insulated sleeping bags, vests, and parkas tend to be particularly popular with canoe campers because they retain much of their insulating value when wet.

Special attention should be paid to sun and insect protection on canoe trips. Canoeists are likely to find little shade on a sunny day, and the glare off the water makes the eyes vulnerable. Carry a sun hat and long cotton clothing as well as good sun cream, and be sure you have a pair of dark glasses. Polarized sunglasses serve rather well against the glare from water. Carry plenty of concentrated insect repellent and consider taking bars of mosquito netting if you don't have a tent that's sealed against insects. Canoe country is bug country.

Fires can be more readily justified on canoe trips than in many other sorts of lightweight camping, since wood often grows quite rapidly in the areas canoeists frequent. Remember that the impact of paddlers tends to be concentrated along a narrow strip of shoreline, however, and be wary of fire danger.

Another pleasant aspect of canoe camping is that groups may include people with widely divergent abilities and strength, provided aims are kept modest. Children can go along as passengers, paddling when they feel the urge. Anyone who's desperate for harder work can always be accommodated—you may go to sleep and let him or her paddle. If you remember that the point of the trip is to have a good time and not to prove how far you can go, you can have a lot of fun canoe camping in a party with members ranging from seasoned veterans to rank beginners.

chapter 20 | **Kayaking**

The kayak is not so versatile a craft as the canoe, but it does have special attractions. It was developed by the Eskimos for hunting in the seas of the far north. The brilliant innovation that made the kayak unique was a completely closed boat with the paddler seated in a sealed cockpit; instead of widening the beam for stability, the Eskimo made it narrower and learned to turn it back up with the leverage of the paddle against the water in case of capsizing. The technique of the "Eskimo roll" is at the heart of most kayaking. The kayak is a superb small boat in rough water. Most canoes are open boats, vulnerable to swamping; the special white-water varieties with permanently closed decks are more akin to kayaks in design than they are to standard canoes.

There are wide kayaks, sometimes accommodating more than one person, which are basically rather stable. They are made for paddling mainly on lakes and easy rivers and aren't designed to be rolled. Though such boats have closed decks and the paddlers sit down and use double paddles, these kayaks tend to have more in common with conventional canoes than with the narrower and tippier kayaks used in white water.

Like canoes, kayaks can be designed for a wide variety of

purposes. Most of the folding kayaks now made are of the large and stable variety, and they make excellent wilderness craft for lakes and gentle rivers. The majority of kayaks used today, however, are short, narrow boats designed for a single paddler. They feel extremely unstable to a novice, because they're made to allow the paddler to lean easily into turns. The kayaker braces the paddle against the river's currents to maintain stability, and the boat is sealed off so that if it tips over, the kayaker can roll back up without taking on any water.

THE WHITE-WATER KAYAK

The usual modern kayak is made with laminates of plastic resin and cloth of fiberglass or synthetic material. The craft has a smooth, rounded hull and deck forming one continuous curve. Such boats are usually just over 13 feet long, the minimum length for organized slalom racing, but those designed for touring or for downriver speed races may be a few feet longer. They're normally just under two feet wide and have loops of rope or webbing installed in each end so that the boat can be easily grabbed in or out of the water. The kayaker sits in a seat placed in a cockpit in the center of the boat, and the rim of the cockpit, or coaming, forms a lip over which the elasticized edge of a spray skirt can be stretched. The spray skirt, made of waterproof fabric or neoprene rubber, is worn by the kayaker around the waist and is shaped to form a deck over the cockpit. It seals out water but permits escape in case of accident.

The white-water kayak is a specialized craft. It's designed to be very maneuverable and to permit boating in extremely turbulent water. There are many subtleties of design, each of which emphasizes one specialized feature over another, particularly in boats intended for competition. You should spend a good deal of time talking to experienced boaters before you

Figure 47 Kayaking permits negotiation of waters ranging from local ponds to thundering rapids. Here a kayaker plays the rapids in a remote wilderness river.

buy a kayak, because minor features in design or construction can make the difference between a boat suitable for a beginner and one that's practically useless except in the hands of an expert. Very often secondhand boats are ideal for beginners. Boats that are termed recreational kayaks and older slalom designs are usually the most suitable kayaks for beginners interested in white-water kayaking.

OTHER EQUIPMENT

Besides the boat and spray skirt, the beginner has to obtain a paddle and a number of other pieces of equipment at an early stage. The paddle is double-bladed, with one blade set at a right angle to the other, so that when the kayaker is paddling, wind resistance from the blade in the air is minimized. The overall length is generally around 84 inches, and the shaft should have a slightly oval cross-section, with the long axis of the oval perpendicular to the blade at each end, allowing the paddler to feel the blade angle. The blades may be flat or slightly curved. If they're curved for efficiency, then the blades can be oriented in one of two ways. depending on whether the paddler controls the angle of the paddle with the right or left hand. Normally, right-handed people choose paddles with right-hand control and left-handed boaters pick left-hand-control paddles.

If practicing is done in a swimming pool or on a warm lake, no additional equipment may be needed while the novice is learning basics. Before going out in a river, into deep water far from shore, or onto cold water, however, you must obtain flotation for the kayak, a life preserver, a wet suit, and a helmet. Wet suits have been discussed already, and the kayaker needs one whenever the weather or the water is chilly; kayakers do not stay dry. For white water, a life preserver and a helmet are essential for safety. You can't do an Eskimo roll if you hit your head on a rock while upside down. A fiberglass kayak sinks if it's filled with water, and in white water it must be kept floating as high as possible to prevent damage. This is most commonly managed by using air-filled bags shaped to fill most of the kayak. The camper normally gets flotation bags that can be opened to store equipment and then sealed and inflated.

LEARNING TO KAYAK

Like climbing, kayaking is a sport that's difficult to learn safely alone. Though it's quite possible to learn to maneuver the boat and to do the Eskimo roll on your own, most people find it far simpler if they're taught by experienced boaters. Actual running of rapids can't be done safely alone, particularly as a beginner, so you may as well get in touch with some good kayakers to begin with. Most instruction is done either in club programs or by kayakers teaching professionally in their spare time. Paid programs may be very good or rather poor, depending on the quality of the instructors. If you pay well for instruction, make sure the credentials of the instructors are good: You may be trusting your life to them. Club programs are usually quite well organized for beginners, but since the instructors are normally donating their time, you should expect basic instruction to take place before the boating season begins. Kayakers aren't likely to give up their weekends to teach rolling in a local lake when they could be running rivers. If you're lucky enough to have friends who are willing to teach you to boat, keep this point in mind. Ask them before the season starts, so that you can learn the basics in time to get out on the river when the runoff starts.

Kayaking technique is too complex to discuss in detail in the limited space available here, but there are several good books listed in the appendix which describe and illustrate all the strokes and ways to maneuver the kayak. The first step in learning is to practice getting into the boat and out of it from shore or the side of a swimming pool, putting on the spray skirt, and getting comfortable with the other paraphernalia. The kayak feels very unstable at first, and just getting accustomed to it takes a couple of sessions in the pool or on the lake. (In many parts of the country, swimming pools are used for most off-season training, since the boating season is often well under way before lakes are warm enough for pleasant practice.)

The novice should spend a couple of hours paddling around, acquiring a feel for the boat, and learning to paddle it straight forward without too much wobbling. Check the braces and be sure they're adjusted so you can hold the boat tightly but comfortably with your feet, legs, and hips. With a secondhand boat that doesn't have movable braces, the positions may have to be changed before the boat fits you properly. At an early stage, you should deliberately tip over a few times and get out of the boat underwater. This is quite easy, but it's important to convince yourself that you can't be trapped in the boat. This also gives you some practice in emptying out water that gets in. Leave the boat upside down until you get it to shore, so that less water enters.

The next stage in learning to kayak is to master the Eskimo roll. Rolling is a tricky skill to learn, and it may take quite a few hours. It's difficult to visualize, and it's also hard to coordinate the muscles even after you understand the principles of the roll. But once learned, rolling is really quite easy. No great physical strength is needed; proper execution and timing are the key. Rolling is critical to white-water boating for a number of reasons. Most of the important strokes used in a swirling river require strong leans. The paddler leans over onto the water, using the paddle for support. In practicing these strokes, a lot of dunkings are bound to result, and it's far too time-consuming to bail out of the kayak every time you lean too far, tow it to shore, empty it out, and get back in. Once you have perfected the roll, all you have to do is turn back up and try again. A strong roll also gives you the confidence you need to lean into your strokes as you should; without it you're afraid to really commit yourself. Once you have developed a really reliable roll, you'll progress very rapidly. Without one, progress will be very slow.

ON THE RIVER

The object of all the practice just outlined is running rivers. White-water boating is one of the most delightful of outdoor sports. The competent kayaker in a set of rapids has the satisfaction of being in the middle of tremendous natural energy. The force of the water rushing by, crashing onto the rocks, swirling and sucking its way downstream is awesome, but there are patterns and a logic to the maelstrom. The kayaker follows the turns of the river down, using the forces of the opposing currents to maneuver the boat, slipping into eddies in the middle of the foam to rest and inspect the course below, and darting back and forth across fast-moving jets of water.

Despite the power of the moving water, kayaking is rarely a daredevil sport. Techniques have been developed over the years to make playing in the rapids quite safe most of the time, and when risks are taken by competent boaters, they're calculated ones. As with any outdoor activity, the safety margin in kayaking is provided by the participants. Kayaking is normally safe because the boaters are, not because there are no potential dangers.

The most important safety rules in kayaking are to know your limits and respect them. Don't boat alone. Some good paddlers occasionally boat by themselves, either running rapids they know they can handle with a wide safety margin or choosing to undertake an additional risk deliberately. Solo boating is rather rare among experienced kayakers, however. For novices, running white water alone is utterly foolhardy. Boat with others, and be sure that they're experienced enough to handle any problems that may arise. Always wear a life preserver, a helmet, and necessary protection against cold water when running rapids. Make sure your boat has adequate flotation. If you have to bail out, keep a hold on the paddle and the boat, and swim for shore or an eddy unless you're in danger; if you are, drop the equipment. Stay upstream of the kayak if you get out; otherwise, it can pin you against a rock. Wear shoes, and swim with your feet downstream to ward off rocks. Trees and log-jams are deadly because the water sweeps under them, and they can catch a swimmer below the surface. Avoid such obstacles at all costs. If you are being carried into one anyway, face downstream, so that if you're caught, you'll tend to wash face up.

The leader of a river party normally designates experienced paddlers as the lead and the sweep. Never go ahead of the lead boat, and never fall behind the sweep. When you're more experienced, you'll learn to assist boaters in trouble, but as a beginner, stay in a safe place and out of the way when a boater needs help. If you're being assisted by another boater when you're in the water, hang onto your equipment and keep swimming. Don't rely solely on the paddler of the rescue boat to get you to shore.

There are a lot of other safety precautions that are too detailed to be presented here. You can learn some of them from the recommended reading, and you'll be taught them when you go out with experienced kayakers. Pay attention to what they say. Kayaking is an exciting and very pleasurable sport, but a good safety margin depends on a group working well together. For beginners, this means doing what you're told by the experienced boaters who are kind enough to take you out.

CAMPING BY KAYAK

The most satisfying of kayak camping trips are those taken down wilderness white-water rivers. These can either be self-contained, with all equipment carried in the kayaks, or with raft support. Beginners will have to practice a good deal on short day trips before undertaking longer white-water trips by kayak. A wide margin of safety is necessary for trips of many days on a remote river. Rescue may be difficult, and the loss of a boat or injury to a member of the party can cause severe and costly inconveniences to the whole group. A mishap may put everyone's safety in jeopardy and may cause difficulties for future kayak parties who want to run the same river. Bureaucrats often tend to be uninformed and skeptical about the ability of kayakers to run difficult rivers. For these reasons and others, you shouldn't expect to start off on multi-day white-water trips until you have had a lot of practice on rapids near the road.

You can have a lot of fun camping with your kayak, however, as soon as you have learned to handle the boat and roll, and you can acquire useful experience at the same time. Camping trips on lakes and slow rivers without real rapids don't require a high degree of expertise, only some common sense and basic camping ability. Any of the trips usually undertaken by lake canoeists are equally feasible in kayaks, though white-water boats are a bit slower than craft made specifically for cruising.

Kayak camping is much like canoe camping, except that the kayaker has to be far more careful about weight and bulk than the canoeist. White-water kayaks are built with a minimum of extra carrying capacity, so the kayak camper has to pare equipment down to essentials. Extra clothing for camp is absolutely essential. Hanging around camp in a cold wet suit is miserable and chilling, once the sun has gone down and you are no longer exercising.

The kayaker must also be particularly careful to protect equipment from getting wet. Kayaks are built low to the water, which is an advantage in the wind. The sealed kayak also doesn't ship water when waves come up, but there's almost always a little bilge water slopping around in the bottom of the boat, and anything that's not sealed tightly will be soaked.

You should pack heavy gear as near the center of the kayak as possible when you're loading the boat. Weight near the ends has to be moved much farther when you're maneuvering the kayak, so it makes the boat sluggish. Load approximately equal weights in either end, so that the kayak will float level in the water. Putting much more weight in one end radically changes the boat's handling.

Kayak camping in easy water helps you prepare for more

challenging white-water trips. The thrill of running wilderness rivers is unlike any other. The river has rightly been a symbol of life throughout human history. Following its course through great canyons and meandering flood plains is a passage along one of the living arteries of the continent.

Appendix:
Where to Get
More Information

This section is intended to give the reader some idea of where to go to look for more detailed advice about particular outdoor activities and for different points of view. Many of the books mentioned contain extensive suggestions for additional reading in the areas they cover, and some of the catalogs offer selections from the literature on outdoor subjects. But the list presented here is a starting point, and it's not at all complete.

Equipment selection for the particular activities mentioned is discussed in most of the books, and some of the catalogs are quite helpful, provided you allow for a natural bias in favor of the gear being offered.

Backpacking

BRIDGE, RAYMOND, *America's Backpacking Book*. New York: Charles Scribner's Sons, 1973.

FLETCHER, COLIN, *The New Complete Walker*. New York: Alfred A. Knopf, 1974.

MANNING, HARVEY, *Backpacking: One Step at a Time*. New York: Random House, 1973.

WINNETT, THOMAS, *Backpacking for Fun.* Berkeley, Calif.: Wilderness Press, 1973.

Cycling

BRIDGE, RAYMOND, *Freewheeling: The Bicycle Camping Book.* Harrisburg, Pa.: Stackpole, 1974.

CUTHBERTSON, TOM, *Anybody's Bike Book.* Berkeley, Calif.: Ten Speed Press, 1971.

DELONG, FRED, *DeLong's Guide to Bicycles and Bicycling.* Radnor, Pa.: Chilton, 1974.

Ski Touring and Snowshoeing

BRIDGE, RAYMOND, *The Complete Snow Camper's Guide.* New York: Charles Scribner's Sons, 1973.

BROWER, DAVID (editor), *Manual of Ski Mountaineering.* San Francisco: Sierra Club, 1962.

FREEMAN, CORTLANDT, *Steve Rieschl's Ski-Touring for the Fun of It.* Boston: Little, Brown and Co., 1974.

LACHAPELLE, EDWARD, *ABC of Avalanche Safety.* Denver: Colorado Outdoor Sports, 1961.

PERLA, RONALD, and MARTINELLI, M., *Avalanche Handbook,* Dept. of Agriculture Handbook 489. Washington, D.C.: U.S. Government Printing Office, 1975.

PRATER, GENE, *Snowshoeing.* Seattle: The Mountaineers, 1975.

Climbing

BRIDGE, RAYMOND, *Climbing: A Guide to Mountaineering.* New York: Charles Scribner's Sons, 1977.

FERBER, PEGGY (editor), *Mountaineering: the Freedom of the Hills*. Seattle: The Mountaineers, 1974.

ROBBINS, ROYAL, *Advanced Rockcraft*. Glendale, Calif.: La Siesta Press, 1973.

ROBBINS, ROYAL, *Basic Rockcraft*. Glendale, Calif.: La Siesta Press, 1971.

Canoeing

AMERICAN RED CROSS, *Canoeing*. Garden City, N.Y.: Doubleday, 1956.

BRIDGE, RAYMOND, *The Complete Canoeist's Guide*. New York: Charles Scribner's Sons, 1978.

DAVIDSON, JAMES WEST, and RUGGE, JOHN, *The Complete Wilderness Paddler*. New York: Alfred A. Knopf, 1976.

Kayaking

BRIDGE, RAYMOND, *The Complete Guide to Kayaking*. New York: Charles Scribner's Sons, 1977.

EVANS, JAY, and ANDERSON, ROBERT, *Kayaking: the New Whitewater Sport for Everybody*. Brattleboro, Vt.: Stephen Greene Press, 1975.

Cooking

BARKER, HARRIETT, *The One-Burner Gourmet*. Matteson, Ill.: Greatlakes Living Press, 1975.

BULTMAN, PHYLLIS, *Two Burners and an Ice Chest: The Art of Relaxed Cooking in a Boat or a Camper or Under the Stars*. Englewood Cliffs, N.J.: Prentice-Hall, 1977.

Routefinding and Weather

DISLEY, JOHN, *Orienteering.* Harrisburg, Pa.: Stackpole, 1973.

KJELLSTROM, BJORN, *Be Expert with Map and Compass.* New York: Charles Scribner's Sons, 1976.

LEHR, PAUL, *et al., Weather.* New York: Golden Press, 1965.

RUTSTRUM, CALVIN, *The Wilderness Route Finder.* New York: Macmillan, 1967.

WATTS, ALAN, *Instant Weather Forecasting.* New York: Dodd, Mead, & Co., 1968.

Emergencies

AMERICAN NATIONAL RED CROSS, *Advanced First Aid and Emergency Care.* Garden City, N.Y.: Doubleday, 1973.

COMMITTEE ON INJURIES, AMERICAN ACADEMY OF ORTHOPAEDIC SURGEONS, *Emergency Care and Transportation of the Sick and Injured.* Chicago, 1971.

FEAR, GENE, *Surviving the Unexpected Wilderness Emergency.* Tacoma, Wash.: Survival Education Association, 1972.

WILKERSON, JAMES (editor), *Medicine for Mountaineering.* Seattle: The Mountaineers, 1967.

Equipment

A concept of currently available equipment can be formed by looking through the catalogs of some of the larger stores specializing in lightweight gear. There are more of these every year, and a complete listing would require almost a book in itself. The names of many suppliers can be found in magazines devoted to various aspects of lightweight camping. Some of these are *Canoe, American Whitewater, Down River, Back-*

packer, Wilderness Camping, Mountain Gazette, Mountain, Climbing, Summit, Off Belay, Bicycling, and *Bike World.* Since few outdoor stores catalog canoes and kayaks because of shipping problems and the like, the best source for an overview of what is available is the issue of *Canoe* each year that surveys the available models.

A few mail-order suppliers with informative or unusual catalogs are listed here:

Eastern Mountain Sports, 1041 Commonwealth Ave., Boston, Mass. 02215

Forrest Mountaineering, 1517 Platte St., Denver, Colo. 80202

Frostline Kits, 452 Burbank St., Broomfield, Colo., 80020

Great Pacific Iron Works, P.O. Box 150, Ventura, Calif. 93001

Holubar, Box 7, Boulder, Colo., 80302

Moor & Mountain, 63 Park St., Andover, Mass. 01810

Northwest River Supplies, P.O. Box 9243, Moscow, Idaho 83843

Recreational Equipment, 1525 11th Ave., Seattle, Wash. 98122

The Ski Hut, 1615 University Ave., Berkeley, Calif. 94703

Touring Cyclist, P.O. Box 4009, Boulder, Colo. 80302

Index